D0051520

MARK DRISCOLL

CONFESSIONS

OF A REFORMISSION REV.

HARD LESSONS FROM AN EMERGING MISSIONAL CHURCH

Mark Driscoll will keep you riveted with his personal and sometimes irreverent account of the planting and growth of Mars Hill Church in Seattle. Be warned—this book is not for the faint of heart! Mark writes in the honest, straightforward, street-level vocabulary of his church's target audience. I found it refreshingly honest, entertaining, and challenging and would highly recommend it to anyone who is serious about trying to reach those who have grown up in a postmodern world.

—*Dr. Gary B. Zustiak, Director of Youth Ministries and Resources, Christ in Youth*

Brutal, honest, attractively offensive, and long overdue! Mark Driscoll courageously reveals the inner workings of his church and his shepherd's heart. This book is a must-read for any pastor who is trying to reach the lost and keep his biblical convictions intact. Mark is a brother who speaks for my generation of emerging leaders. He boldly goes where no shepherd has gone before.

—*Grant Fishbook, Christ the King Community Church*

For some, this book will inspire and energize you to keep going as a church on a mission for Jesus. For others, it may rekindle the sense of passion and mission you lost years ago. For others, it may awaken you to the realization that you have only been going through the motions of church and never really experienced the joy of serving Jesus as a missional church. Whatever the case, after reading this book, you will never go back to being an inwardly focused church without a mission.

—*Dan Kimball, author of* The Emerging Church

I walked with Mark as a friend through many of the stories in this book. Reading it was a great reminder of how faithful our God is. Mark gives the straight story on his journey in church-planting, pulling no punches. This book is a great encouragement to anyone wanting to plant a church or living in the trenches of ministry.

—*Rick McKinley, Pastor, Imago Dei Community; author of* Jesus in the Margins

Mark combines penetrating insights into effective biblical ministry in the emerging culture with a deeply personal portrait of his struggles to learn how to be a pastor. People with a passion to be missional will resonate with Mars Hill Church's story of implementing their vision to create a healthy body of believers in the least-churched city in the least-churched state in the country.

—*Gerry Breshears, Professor of Theology, Western Seminary*

Most pastors should not write confessions or memoirs before they have many years of experience in the ministry. Mark Driscoll is clearly an exception. I pray these important lessons from his rather amazing journey will not only serve the vision of his peers but also jar a multitude of ministers to pursue reformission as the church engages our radically changing culture.

—*John H. Armstrong, President, ACT 3*

Since 2000, the congregation that's home to mostly formerly unchurched, hip, media-savvy twenty- to thirty-somethings has increased sixfold.... Exponential growth is one reason why Mars Hill is our "One to Watch" church.

—*Outreach Magazine*

PC is not in this pastor's playbook, and in famously secular Seattle, his Mars Hill Church in Ballard is drawing thousands weekly. His message is fundamentalist Christian, his delivery system is pure alternative culture wired for sound.

—*Seattle Magazine*

Other Books by Mark Driscoll

The Radical Reformission: Reaching Out without Selling Out

The Leadership Network Innovation Series

Confessions of a Reformission Rev.: Hard Lessons from an Emerging Missional Church, Mark Driscoll

The Multi-Site Church Revolution: Being One Church in Many Locations, Geoff Surratt, Greg Ligon, and Warren Bird

The Big Idea: Focus the Message, Multiply the Impact, Dave Ferguson, Jon Ferguson, and Eric Bramlett.

Leadership from the Inside Out: Examining the Inner Life of a Healthy Church Leader, Kevin Harney

Sticky Church, Larry Oborne

MARK DRISCOLL

CONFESSIONS
OF A REFORMISSION REV.

HARD LESSONS FROM AN EMERGING MISSIONAL CHURCH

ZONDERVAN®

ZONDERVAN.com/
AUTHORTRACKER
follow your favorite authors

We want to hear from you. Please send your comments about this book to us in care of zreview@zondervan.com. Thank you.

ZONDERVAN

Confessions of a Reformission Rev.
Copyright © 2006 by Mark Driscoll

Requests for information should be addressed to:
Zondervan, *Grand Rapids, Michigan 49530*

Library of Congress Cataloging-in-Publication Data

Driscoll, Mark.
    Confessions of a reformission rev. : hard lessons from an emerging missional church / Mark Driscoll.
       p. cm. — (The leadership network innovation series)
    Includes bibliographical references.
    ISBN 978-0-310-27016-4
    1. Driscoll, Mark, 1970- 2. Evangelists—United States—Biography.
    3. Mars Hill Church (Seattle, Wash.)—History. I. Title. II. Series.
    BV3785.D75A3   2006
    280'.4—dc22   2005032306

Photography: Thomas James Hurst
Interior design: Beth Shagene

Printed in the United States of America

12 13 14 15 16 17 18 /DCI/ 33 32 31 30 29 28 27 26 25 24 23 22 21 20 19 18 17 16

Contents

Acknowledgments

I want to thank the following people for their insights, which helped to shape this book:

God the Ghost has repeatedly saved me from myself.

Bob Buford, Linda Stanley, and Dave Travis of Leadership Network have generously invested in me since the early days of our church.

Jon Phelps of DC–3 Entertainment has been a mentor in ways of which he is unaware.

Gib Martin is a wonderful encouragement as my father-in-law.

My first pastor, Doug Busby, gave me a love for Scripture, Jesus, and the church.

Ed Stetzer has helped clarify my understanding of missiology.

Tim Keller and John Piper have been insightful theological mentors.

Larry Osborne has graciously contributed insights into my life and church.

The Mars Hill elders are great brothers for making sanctified trouble.

My brothers in Acts 29 are a constant source of inspiration.

My research assistant, Crystal, spent numerous hours preparing the endnotes for this book.

John Vaughan kindly shared his vast knowledge of megachurches.

My wife, Grace, a.k.a. "Beauty," and our five kids are the best part of my life.

Have fun reading my daddy's book.

Prelude

I sure hope this book helps your ministry.

I have made so many mistakes as a pastor that I should be pumping gas for a living instead of preaching the gospel. This book is my telling of the blow-by-blow history of Mars Hill Church, which we planted in Seattle, the great city that I love like a drunk uncle. We named the church after the place where Paul preached to the great pagan city of Athens with cultural relevance by quoting their poets and artists. In retrospect, the name of our church is kind of dumb and sounds more like a cult than a church, which, sad to say, actually benefits us in a city where words like *Jesus* and *Christian* are far more offensive than four-letter cuss words.

When we started Mars Hill, I was in my midtwenties, with a handful of people and about six years of faith in Christ to draw on. We had the crazy dream of making a difference in one of the nation's least-churched cities, where only 8 percent of the population is evangelical Christian and 86 percent does not attend a worship service of any religion during an average week.[1]

Today our dream is alive and well. Our church attendance is running over 4,000 people a week. Of the more than 400,000 churches in the United States, we are among the sixty fastest-growing churches according to *Outreach* magazine, and one of the twenty-five most influential churches in America according to a survey conducted by John Vaughan and reported in *The Church Report*.[2] In saying this, I am not boasting but rather pointing out the obvious miracle of God that we are a part of. In fact, my previous ministry experience would not fill up a three-by-five-inch notecard. Basically, we are a kite in God's hurricane, which is an absolute joke for reasons that will become apparent as you read through the book.

We started the church to fill what I saw as the gap of eighteen-to thirty-five-year-olds who were missing from the churches in our region. It seemed that young people went to church with their parents but upon graduation from high school often dropped out of church altogether, with some returning once they were older, married, and had children. The Holy Spirit burdened me to start a church for the people who had fallen into that dropout hole. Over the years, the statistics have further verified the need for this focus. George Barna says, "Many twentysomethings are reversing course after having been active church attenders during their teenage years. As teenagers, more than half attended church each week and more than 4 out of 5 (81%) had ever gone to a Christian church. That means that from high school graduation to age 25 there is a 42% drop in weekly church attendance and a 58% decline from age 18 to age 29. That represents about 8,000,000 twentysomethings alive today who were active church-goers as teenagers but who will no longer be active in a church by their 30th birthday."[3]

Today, though we are thankfully seeing an increase in older people, the average age at Mars Hill remains in the midtwenties. Through painful trial and error, we have been able to motivate and mobilize younger people for ministry. This is highly unusual. According to Barna, "The research, conducted with 2,660 twenty-somethings, shows that Americans in their twenties are significantly less likely than any other age group to attend church services, to donate to churches, to be absolutely committed to Christianity, to read the Bible, or to serve as a volunteer or lay leader in churches."[4] Barna also says, "Perhaps the most striking reality of twentysome-thing's faith is their relative absence from Christian churches. Only three out of ten twentysomethings (31%) attend church in a typi-cal week, compared to four out of ten of those in their 30s (42%) and nearly half of all adults age 40 and older (49%). The research shows that church attendance bottoms out during the late 20s when the vast majority of students have transitioned from education to the workforce. Just 22% of those ages 25 to 29 attended church in the last week."[5]

An additional oddity is that although we presently average more than two weddings a week, the majority of those at our church are single, since the tendency is to get saved while single and then get married as Christians. In comparison, most churches our size have less than 20 percent singles.[6] According to Barna, "Married people are more likely than singles to attend church in a typical weekend: 53% versus 37% respectively."[7]

Though Mars Hill is peculiar, I do believe it is like one of the doves Noah sent out of the ark to look for land. The Christian church has a new world of ministry opportunity to explore, among cities, young people, and cultural progressives. At one time, cultural trends primarily started on the East and West coasts (e.g., New York and Los Angeles) and then spread toward the center of the country. But today multiple cultural centers from which culture making emanates are scattered in urban centers throughout the country.[8] These cultural centers are marked by such things as airports that provide mobility, vital arts communities, tech-friendly lifestyles, colleges and universities, and blue politics (Democrats).

The urban tribes of culture making and trend setting attract the same people our church attracts, namely, the young, single, educated, creative, and liberal. According to William Frey, between 1995 and 2000, young people ages twenty-five to thirty-four migrated into these cultural centers in the following order:

Atlanta, Georgia
Dallas, Texas
Phoenix, Arizona
Denver, Colorado
Las Vegas, Nevada
Charlotte, North Carolina
Portland, Oregon
Minneapolis, Minnesota
Washington, D.C.
and my city, Seattle, Washington[9]

Conversely, the following ten cities saw the largest number of young people ages twenty-five to thirty-four leave, taking with them valuable human capital and future opportunity for those cities:

Los Angeles, California	Virginia Beach, Virginia
New York, New York	Pittsburgh, Pennsylvania
Miami, Florida	Buffalo, New York
Honolulu, Hawaii	Boston, Massachusetts
San Diego, California	Nassau, New York[10]

Because the magnet cities for culture makers draw some of the best and brightest young people in large numbers (e.g., Seattle gained 27,201 twenty-five- to thirty-four-year-olds between 1995 and 2000), they are increasingly becoming states unto themselves and creating the trends in the regions surrounding them.[11] Therefore, to best prepare for the next wave of ministry opportunity, it is important for Christians to learn from the Noah's-dove churches that are already exploring these new opportunities. God is using young leaders to plant churches in these strategic culture-making urban centers, which often grow into megachurches as they learn to effectively reach the emerging culture. Along with Mars Hill, this would include North Point Community Church (Andy Stanley) outside of Atlanta (www.northpoint.org), Fellowship Bible Church (Ed Young Jr.) in Dallas (www.fellowshipchurch.com), Village Baptist Church (Matt Chandler) in Dallas (www.thevillagechurch. net), The Fellowship Church (Ted Baird) near Phoenix (www .fellowshipanthem.org), Central Christian Church (Jud Wilhite) in Las Vegas (www.centralchristian.com), Imago Dei Church (Rick McKinley) in Portland (www.imagodeicommunity.com), and Covenant Life Church (Joshua Harris) outside of Washington, D.C. (www.covlife.org).

The following chapters recount our painful efforts to plant an emerging church to reach emerging cultures in Seattle. My hope is that our hardships and lessons will help to serve others who are undertaking similar missions and inspire the planting and renewing of many churches to reach emerging cultures.

CHAPTER ZERO

Ten Curious Questions

This book is about the hard lessons we have learned at Mars Hill Church in Seattle (www.marshillchurch.org). Writing this book caused me to reflect on our past and subsequently conjured up a horrendous feeling eerily similar to seeing my high school yearbook photo in which I sported a soccer-rocker mullet. Like me, most people prefer not to dwell on past moments of folly, embarrassment, or failure. But the providential hand of a gracious God commonly uses exactly such occasions to shape ministers and their ministries. At each step of the crazy journey God has had us on, we have made mistakes that should have killed us. But God has continually saved us from ourselves and, like the perfect Father that he is, has taught us important lessons.

Before we get started, I want to ask you a handful of questions that I continually ask myself to ensure that our church remains faithful to Jesus and his mission in our city. These questions will help provide us a common jargon for understanding one another. They are intended to help clarify your church's identity, gospel, mission, size, and priorities.

Question 1

Will your Rev. require reformission?

In my previous book, *The Radical Reformission: Reaching Out without Selling Out*, I explained the growing reformation of what it means to be a Christian missionary.[1] Missions once solely meant sending American Christians into foreign lands and cultures to live among the people there and to bring the gospel of Jesus Christ to them in a relevant way. But reformission also seeks to determine how Christians and their churches can most effectively be missionaries to their own local cultures.

Reformission, therefore, begins with a simple return to Jesus, who, by grace saves us and sends us into reformission. Jesus has called us to (1) the gospel (loving our Lord), (2) the culture (loving our neighbor), and (3) the church (loving our Christian brothers and sisters). One of the causes for the lack of reformission in the American church is that various Christian traditions are prone to faithfulness on only one or two of these counts. Consequently, when we fail to love the Lord, our culture, and our church simultaneously, reformation ceases, leaving one of three holes: the parachurch, liberalism, and fundamentalism.

Gospel + Culture – Church = Parachurch

First, some people become so frustrated with the church that they bring the gospel into culture without it. This is referred to as the *parachurch* and includes evangelistic ministries such as Young Life and Campus Crusade for Christ. The parachurch has a propensity to love the Lord and love its neighbors but not to love the church.

Culture + Church – Gospel = Liberalism

Second, some churches are so concerned with being culturally relevant that, though they are deeply involved in the culture, they neglect the gospel. This is classic liberal Christianity. Liberal Christians run the risk of loving their neighbors and their Christian brothers and sisters at the expense of loving their Lord and his gospel.

Church + Gospel – Culture = Fundamentalism

Third, some churches are more into their church and its traditions, buildings, and politics than they are the gospel. Though they know the gospel theologically, they rarely take it out of their church. This is classic fundamentalist Christianity, which flourishes most widely in more independent-minded, Bible-believing churches. Fundamental Christians are prone to love their Lord and their brothers and sisters but not their neighbors.

The only way out of these holes is repentance, which enables reformission. Through repentance, Christians and churches are empowered by the Holy Spirit to simultaneously love the Lord, love their neighbors, and love their Christian brothers and sisters.

Gospel + Culture + Church = Reformission

Reformission combines the best aspects of each of these types of Christianity: living in the tension of being culturally liberal yet theologically conservative Christians and churches who are absolutely driven by the gospel of grace to love their Lord, their neighbors, and their fellow Christians. This book is a painfully honest chronological account of our church's reformission and how it caused us to grow from 0 to 4,000 people in eight years.

Question 2

Will your church be traditional and institutional, contemporary and evangelical, or emerging and missional?

For the past one thousand years, the Western church has enjoyed a privileged position in the center of culture, during what was known as Christendom. Because of this, the church also provided a common moral framework and language for our nation. Simple examples would include the frequent biblical allusions in the writings of our founding fathers and, more recently, the deeply biblical imagery in the speeches of Martin Luther King Jr.

During the era of Christendom, it was generally believed that our national culture was Christian, or at least Judeo-Christian. Consequently, it was the job of the church to make converts for the nation by challenging people to commit themselves to Jesus and live morally. The upside of Christendom was that many people did attend church. The downside was that the church in large part became the servant of morality and the national good. The result was a mean-spirited hypocrisy among "Christians" who wrongly believed morality and redemption were synonymous and lived lives more dominated by the American values of pride and selfishness than by the gospel virtues of humility and selflessness. Also, Christendom churches defined themselves in contrast to other competing churches, which often led to unnecessary hostility between Christian traditions that were distinct but not altogether different.

The era of Christendom was dominated by the *traditional and institutional church*, which is marked by the following traits:[2]

* Missions is solely funding Americans to evangelize in foreign countries.
* Culture is where the church expects to occupy a privileged position of influence.
* The primary culture to reach is modern.
* Theology is liberalism or fundamentalism, with fighting between the two sides.
* Churches exist largely to meet the needs of church members.
* Churches grow through births and attracting people with denominational loyalties.
* Community means the church is a subculture that is closed to outsiders.
* Pastors are selected and trained in seminaries, outside of the local church.
* Pastors are servants and teachers who do most of the church ministry, especially evangelization of the lost.
* Lost people are not frequently pursued for evangelistic relationships.
* Faith is private and personal.
* Worship services are based on tradition (e.g., robes, hymnals, organs, liturgy)
* Church buildings are considered sacred places (e.g., crosses, stained glass, icons) where people are to dress and act formally.

As the era of Christendom began to wind down, it became apparent that two things were needed. First, the dwindling remnant of Christendom included many people who attended church but did not know Jesus and needed to be saved. Second, the growing baby-boom generation was less likely to attend church and less attracted by tradition or the denominational heritage than their parents had been. The result was the birth of a new form of church, the contemporary and evangelical church, which sought to evangelize the unsaved in the church and to bring other unsaved to the church to be evangelized. Today, the traditional and institutional church is hemorrhaging to death. In 1906, 40 percent of all Sunday worshipers were in mainline denominations.[3] By 1999, that number had fallen to only 16 percent of all worshipers because less people were attending church and those who did were choosing the newer form of church.[4]

The end of Christendom and the transition to a post-Christian culture is currently dominated by the *contemporary and evangelical church*, which is marked by the following common traits:

- Missions is a church department that sends people and money to foreign countries.
- Culture is where the church battles to regain a lost position of privileged influence.
- The primary culture to reach was modern and is transitioning to postmodern.
- Theology is conservative and is built on a modernistic view of truth and knowledge.
- Churches exist to meet the felt needs of spiritual consumers.
- Churches grow through marketing that brings people to church events.
- Community means the church is a safe subculture that welcomes lost people into the church.
- Pastors need not have formal theological training or ordination.

- Pastors are CEOs who lead and manage their staff, which is responsible for ministry.
- Lost people are invited to evangelistic church programs that target seekers.
- Faith is private and personal but is openly shown at church.
- Worship services are based on styles from the 1980s and 1990s (acoustic guitars, drama, etc.).
- Church buildings are functional places (e.g., no crosses, no stained glass, no icons) where people can dress and act informally.

With Christendom essentially winding down now in the United States and officially over in Europe, the traditional and institutional church is dying as its market share dries up, and the contemporary and evangelical church is scrambling to adjust to emerging postmodern cultures and generations. A third incarnation of the church is arising, the *emerging and missional church*, which is marked by the following traits:

- Missions is every Christian being a missionary to their local culture.
- The church accepts that it is marginalized in culture and holds no privileged position of influence but gains influence by serving the common good.
- The primary culture to reach is postmodern and pluralistic.
- Theology ranges from ancient orthodoxy to heterodox liberalism built on postmodern denials of true truth and known knowledge.
- Churches are the people who love Jesus and serve his mission in a local culture.
- Churches grow as Christians bring Jesus to lost people through hospitality.
- Community means the church is a counterculture with a new kingdom way of life through Jesus.

- Pastors need not be ordained or formally educated in theology and are trained in the church.
- Pastors are missiologists who train Christians to be effective missionaries.
- Lost people are saved by the Holy Spirit when and how he determines.
- Faith is lived publicly together as the church and includes all of life.
- Worship services blend ancient forms and current local cultural styles.
- Church buildings are sacred, as is all of God's creation.

Because the declining, dominant, and emerging church types each work from a different set of assumptions, it is incredibly important that churches and church leaders determine which church form they will adopt. And to answer this question, they must carefully consider what the people in their local culture are like. For example, a church ministering to modern-thinking retirees would likely have better success with a traditional and institutional church. This explains why Coral Ridge Presbyterian Church, with a traditional liturgy, a robed choir, a pipe organ, and the classic oration of preacher Dr. James Kennedy, is flourishing among retirees in Florida. Conversely, a church ministering to suburban baby boomers would likely have better success with a contemporary and evangelical church, such as Willow Creek or Saddleback, and a pastor like Rick Warren or Bill Hybels. And a church ministering to spiritual young creative types would likely have better success with an emerging and missional church and pastor.

This book is about our church, Mars Hill, which is an emerging and missional church because that is the most effective church form for reaching the city of Seattle, to which God has called us. I believe that the emerging and missional church will eventually displace the contemporary and evangelical church in much the same way that it displaced the traditional and institutional church. But as long as there are varying cultures of people, there will be multiple church forms.

The point is not that one of these church forms is good and the others are bad. Rather, one is likely more effective for reaching the people in your local culture than the other forms are. Therefore, those using one church form need not critique the other forms as long as all are faithful to the functions mandated for the church in Scripture.

To be effective, churches and their leaders must first evaluate what type of church they presently are. Churches must also evaluate what their culture will look like in the future and how their church can best prepare to reach that emerging culture. They must then become the church that their future culture will need, if they are not already.

Question 3

Will your church be an emergent liberal church or an emerging evangelical church?

I was part of what is now known as the Emerging Church Movement in its early days and spent a few years traveling the country to speak to emerging leaders in an effort to help build a missional movement in the United States. The wonderful upside of the emerging church is that it elevates mission in American culture to a high priority, which is a need so urgent that its importance can hardly be overstated.

I had to distance myself, however, from one of many streams in the emerging church because of theological differences. Since the late 1990s, this stream has become known as Emergent. The emergent church is part of the Emerging Church Movement but does not embrace the dominant ideology of the movement. Rather, the emergent church is the latest version of liberalism. The only difference is that the old liberalism accommodated modernity and the new liberalism accommodates postmodernity.

During dinner one evening with a friend, Dan Kimball, who wrote *The Emerging Church*, I was struck by his distinction between the emergent church and the emerging church.[5] There has been much confusion on this matter, partly due to the similarity in names. The emerging church is a growing, loosely connected movement of primarily young pastors who are glad to see the end of modernity and are seeking to function as missionaries who bring the gospel of Jesus Christ to emerging and postmodern cultures. The emerging church welcomes the tension of holding in one closed hand the unchanging truth of evangelical Christian theology (Jude 3) and holding in one open hand the many cultural ways of showing and speaking Christian truth as a missionary to America (1 Cor. 9:19–23). Since the movement, if it can be called that, is young and is still defining its theological center, I do not want to portray the movement as ideologically unified because I myself swim in the theologically conservative stream of the emerging church.

I am particularly concerned, however, with some growing trends among some people: the rejection of Jesus' death on the cross as a penal substitute for our sins;[6] resistance to openly denouncing homosexual acts as sinful;[7] the questioning of a literal eternal torment in hell, which is a denial that holds up only until, in an ironic bummer, you die and find yourself in hell;[8] the rejection of God's sovereignty over and knowledge of the future, as if God were a junior-college professor who knows only bits and pieces of trivia;[9] the rejection of biblically defined gender roles, thereby contributing to the "mantropy" epidemic among young guys now fretting over the best kind of looffah for their skin type and the number of women in the military dying to save their Bed, Bath and Beyond from terrorist attacks;[10] and the rejection of biblical names for God, such as Father, which is essentially apologizing before the unbelieving world for the prayer life of the flamboyantly heterosexual Jesus, who uttered the horrendously politically incorrect "Our Father" without ever having the decency to apologize for being a misogynist patriarchal meanie.[11] This is ultimately all the result of a diminished respect for the perfection, authority, and clarity of Scripture, all of which was written by patriarchal men. After all, how in the world can we possibly know what anything means after we have a college degree?[12] Come to think of it, I'm not even sure what I mean when I say that I'm not sure what Scripture means—know what I mean?

For some Emergent leaders, this critique may be as welcome as water on a cat. But I assure you that I speak as one within the Emerging Church Movement who has great love and appreciation for Christian leaders with theological convictions much different from my own. And because the movement has defined itself as a conversation, I would hope there would be room in the conversation for those who disagree, even poke a bit of fun, but earnestly desire to learn from and journey with those also striving to be faithful to God and fruitful in emerging cultures. Standing with my brothers and sisters in our great mission, I hope this book can in some small way help the greater church emerge in biblical faithfulness and missional fruitfulness.

Therefore, it is very important that any church seeking to be emerging define whether it is an emerging evangelical church or an emergent liberal church. Our church is emerging and missional in its practice and evangelical and biblical in its theology.

Question 4

Will you proclaim a gospel of forgiveness, fulfillment, or freedom?

Traditional, contemporary, and emerging churches also differ in how they present the gospel. The traditional church generally proclaims a gospel of forgiveness. According to the gospel of forgiveness, we have sinned against God and are under his wrath until we ask for his forgiveness and live changed lives of repentance. This gospel worked for people in Christendom because they had a general knowledge of authority, sin, judgment, hell, and Jesus.

Though this gospel made sense to most people at one time, this sort of gospel seems judgmental, mean-spirited, naive, and narrow-minded to the ever-growing number of people who do not understand the basic tenets of Christianity. Such people do not appreciate being pushed to make an immediate decision to reject sin and accept Jesus because they don't know what sin is or who Jesus is until we have taken the time to inform their understanding, which may take months or years in a friendship.

The contemporary church generally proclaims a gospel of fulfillment. This gospel is influenced by the non-Christian psychologist Abraham Maslow and his hierarchy of needs.[13] His point is that people move from basic survival needs to higher needs of actualizing their full potential to be and do all that they desire. The problem with Maslow's theory is simple but significant. He establishes each individual human being as their own god, on their own mission, pursuing their own glory. In this framework, I do not exist for God but rather God exists for me. For example, if the Lord's Prayer were rewritten according to Maslow's priorities, it would read "My kingdom come, my will be done, for mine is the kingdom, power, and glory."

The contemporary church's gospel of fulfillment essentially accepts Maslow's faulty hierarchy and teaches that God exists to enable each of us to actualize our full potential. So in this therapeutic gospel, you use Jesus to achieve your ends, which can vary from health to wealth to emotional contentment, or whatever personal vision you have for your own glory.[14] What hinders the fulfillment of our full potential is not that we are sinners but rather that we don't love ourselves enough and don't have enough self-esteem and positive thinking. God exists to worship us, by telling us how loveable we are and how valuable we are. In this gospel, the cross is an echo of my own great worth, since God found me so loveable and so valuable that he was willing to die for me so that I could love myself, believe in myself, and achieve my full glory.

The therapeutic gospel is a false gospel and an enemy of mission for many reasons. First, it does not call me to love God and my neighbor, but instead only to love myself. Second, it does not call me to God's mission but rather calls God to my mission. Third, it does not call me to be part of the church to serve God's mission, but instead to use the church to make me a better person. Fourth, it does not call me to use my spiritual gift(s) to build up the church but rather to actualize my full potential. Fifth, it takes pride, which Augustine called the mother of all sins, and repackages it as self-esteem, the maidservant of all virtue.

The emerging church proclaims a gospel of freedom. According to the gospel of freedom, we were made to live in community with God and with each other without the pains of sin and death. But because of our sin, we have wrecked God's good creation and brought death and havoc into all of life. And though we are self-destructive, God in his loving-kindness has chosen to save us from ourselves. Our God, Jesus, came to live without sin as our example, die for our sin as our substitute, and rise from death as our Lord who liberates us from Satan, sin, and death.

The gospel of freedom says that only through Jesus can we be brought back into friendship with God and with each other, because he takes away the sin that separates us. And only through Jesus can we be brought back into his original intentions for us: worshiping God instead of ourselves, serving the common good, making culture, and through his grace, helping to right what has been made wrong through sin. The Bible is replete with the gospel of freedom, beginning with Moses. Perhaps the most obvious example is found in the story of the Exodus, from which Paul adopts his understanding of redemption to mean being freed by God from slavery to evil.

Question 5

Will your church be attractional, missional, or both?

The contemporary church growth movement and its evangelical seeker churches are attraction-based, meaning that the church functions as a purveyor of religious goods and services. Therefore, the primary task of these churches is to bring people from the culture into the church to partake of programming that targets their felt needs.

Conversely, emerging and missional churches see the church's primary task as sending Christians out of the church and into the culture to serve as missionaries through relationships, rather than bringing lost people into the church to be served by programming. Pastors of emerging and missional churches routinely criticize the attraction-based model as caring only about bringing more people in to grow a bigger church. And pastors of attraction-based churches commonly defend themselves by stating that their churches are larger than most emerging and missional churches, which they say proves that attraction-based churches are more effectively making disciples as Jesus commanded.

The growing criticism between these camps is in large part unnecessary, because they are working for the same goal—the reaching of lost people for Jesus—but simply using different methods, methods that are complimentary, not contradictory. Consequently, churches must both bring people in and send people out and must therefore structure themselves to achieve both objectives. Additionally, we see both attractional and missional ministry methods in the life of Jesus Christ.

Jesus' incarnation is in itself missional. God the Father sent God the Son into culture on a mission to redeem the elect by the power of God the Ghost. After his resurrection, Jesus also sent his disciples into culture, on a mission to proclaim the success of his mission, and commissioned all Christians to likewise be missionaries to the cultures of the world (e.g., Matt. 28:18–20; John 20:21; Acts 1:7–8). Emerging and missional Christians have wonderfully rediscovered the significance of Jesus' incarnational example of being a missionary immersed in a culture.

But sadly, they are also prone to overlook the attractional nature of Jesus' earthly ministry.[15] In addition to immersing himself in a culture for a mission, Jesus' ministry was also marked by the large crowds that were drawn to him because of his preaching and miracles.

One important example of the attractional elements of Jesus' ministry is found in the sixth chapter of John's gospel. A very large crowd, numbering thousands of people, came to see Jesus perform miracles and to hear him preach. Jesus appears to be modeling attractional church growth strategies of doing what was needed to gather many people to hear the preaching of the gospel. Jesus then fed the entire crowd by miraculously multiplying a little boy's lunch, which would only have increased the crowds that thronged to see him.

But Jesus then preached that he was the bread of life, which drove many people away from him in confusion and disagreement. We see that Jesus not only gathered a crowd but also intentionally drove many people away because they were not among the elect chosen for salvation (John 6:37). Some disciples, however, remained with Jesus and continued to be trained as missionaries by Jesus. They were later sent out to follow his pattern of incarnating in a culture, attracting crowds, preaching hard words that harden some hearts and soften others, and then training those who believe to be missionaries who follow Jesus' principles of attractional and missional ministry.

Therefore, the growing hostility between attractional-ministry pastors with larger churches and missional-ministry pastors with smaller churches need not occur. Instead, each needs to learn from the other; each has a vital piece of the truth gleaned from the life of Jesus.

Attractional churches need to transform their people from being consumers in the church to being missionaries outside of the church. Missional churches need to gather crowds to their church so that hard words of repentance can be preached in an effort to expose people's hearts. Those whom God saves can then be trained to go back out into the culture as missionaries to gather more people to repeat the process. Simply, the goal of a church that is both missional and attractional is to continually follow Jesus' example so that more people are saved for God's mission and more influence is spread for God's kingdom, without rejecting one aspect of Jesus' ministry in favor of another.

Question 6

What size shoe will your church wear?

Churches, like children, have a shoe size that they will grow into. As a church grows, it must accept its size. This can be difficult because people have different ideas of what constitutes "large" and "small." Additionally, people are prone to attach a moral value to church size. This means that people who prefer a small church will criticize a large church for being too slick and impersonal, and people who prefer a big church will criticize a small church for not experiencing enough conversion growth, diversity of people, or quality of programming.

When it comes to church size, a few things are important to remember. First, a church must determine what size they would like to become and start acting like a church of that size if they hope to achieve that goal. Second, a church must accept its size and not allow people to demand that they receive the type of treatment they would receive at a church of whatever size they prefer. An example of this would be the expectation of some people in a large church that the pastor be as accessible as the pastor of a smaller church. Third, for a church to grow, it must also accept that the church will change. The problem with most churches is not that they don't want to experience conversion growth but rather that they do not want to change, which negates their ability to grow and is a sin to be repented of.

Therefore, each church must ask how large they want to be and prepare to work toward that goal. To help determine a reasonable goal, it is helpful to see the various sizes of other churches. However, determining size categories for churches is very difficult. The following is a rough estimate I came up with after reading some books on the subject[16] and interviewing John Vaughan of Church Growth Today, who was particularly helpful. No one is exactly sure how many Protestant churches there are in the United States, but the general figures are somewhere between 400,000 and 500,000 churches.[17] So for purposes of a rough estimate, I am assuming that there are 400,000 Protestant churches in the United States. I am also assuming that the reported attendance at these churches is accurate, which is highly questionable since the overreporting of church attendance is estimated by some to be as high as 50 percent.[18] Therefore, a rough estimate of weekly church attendance for adults and children in America breaks down as follows:

Churches with 45 people or less	100,000 churches, 25% of all churches
Churches with 75 people or less	200,000 churches, 50% of all churches
Churches with 150 people or less	300,000 churches, 75% of all churches
Churches with 350 people or less	380,000 churches, 95% of all churches
Churches with 800 people or less	392,000 churches, 98% of all churches
Churches with 800 people or *more*	8,000 churches, 2% of all churches
Churches with 2,000 people or *more*	870 churches, 0.22% of all churches
Churches with 3,000 people or *more*	425 churches, 0.11% of all churches

Summarily, George Barna says, "Four out of ten church-going adults (41%) go to churches with 100 or fewer adults while about one out of eight church-going adults (12%) can be found in churches of 1000 or more adults."[19]

According to church expert Lyle Schaller, the two most comfortable church sizes are 45 people or less and 150 people or less.[20] Consequently, these are likely also the hardest size barriers a pastor has to push through. Practically, it seems that churches of 45 people or less are large enough to gather for worship and function as a church but small enough for everyone to know each other and have a say in everything that happens. A congregation of 150 or less can usually gather in one service and exist as one community, yet have the resources to hire a pastor to care for all the people. These factors may help explain why the average church in America is reportedly 89 people.[21]

Pushing through the 350 barrier can also be very difficult, because it usually requires that the church transition to multiple pastors, multiple services, and multiple communities. The following chapters will speak very practically of how we navigated through each of these seasons, from being a church of under 45 people to being a church of over 4,000 people. I acknowledge that some readers may be turned off by my focus on numbers, even though we have a book of the Bible titled the same word. But every number is a person, so numbers do matter because people matter.

A megachurch is technically 2,000 or more adults and children in weekly worship.[22] The first modern megachurch was led by my favorite Christian outside of the Bible, Charles Haddon Spurgeon, whose church grew to more than 5,000 people in London in the late nineteenth century.[23] Perhaps the first megachurch in America was led by the aberrant theologian Charles Finney, who preached to between 2,000 and 3,000 people each week at Chatham Street Chapel in New York City in the late nineteenth century.[24] In 1970, there were only 10 non-Catholic megachurches in the United States.[25] Today there are more than 1,000 U. S. megachurches, and a new church breaks the 2,000-attendance threshold every 2 days, according to megachurch expert John Vaughan.[26]

But emerging and missional churches will include more megachurches than ever, and they will be both attractional and missional in their philosophy of ministry. If a church is truly missional, it may become a megachurch for three reasons: (1) the power of the gospel of Jesus Christ is powerful and effective, (2) a truly outward-focused missional church will experience conversion growth, and (3) a truly missional church has such a burning desire for cultural transformation that it must grow large enough to serve a whole city. Mars Hill is one of the first emerging and missional megachurches in the country to target postmodern culture.

Schaller notes that most people born after 1965 are used to functioning in much larger institutions (e.g., schools, grocery stores, hardware stores).[27] Therefore, younger people generally feel at home in larger churches, which partially explains the popularity of megachurches and the willingness of younger people to drive greater distances to attend a megachurch.

Schaller's teaching and our experience at Mars Hill confirms that emerging generations indeed feel more comfortable in larger churches. This information runs contrary to much of the popular teaching today, which asserts that the future of the church will be house churches and smaller church communities. I believe that the megachurch phenomenon is not over but rather just beginning, that the "experts" are simply wrong, and that the future trend will be toward the extremes of very small and very large churches.

Nothing is wrong with a small church, providing it hates sin, loves Jesus, serves people, obeys Scripture, and sees transformed lives. However, I find the conversation among numerous young pastors who prefer smaller churches to be theologically troubling. The governing assumption is that the early church, described in Acts, was not a megachurch with systems and structures but simply small groups of Christians hanging out informally in one another's homes.

This position was reinforced in a conversation I had with Michael Frost and Alan Hirsch, who wrote the popular and insightful book *The Shaping of Things to Come*.[28] During a lecture they gave in the Seattle area, they stressed this point and referenced the account of Acts 2:42–47, in which the early church is described as small, disorganized, and meeting informally in homes. But what they failed to also note is that in those same verses, the early church did meet in a larger gathering in the temple courts. And in Acts 2:41, God added three thousand converts in one day, making the early church an immediate megachurch. Curiously, this was accomplished by a good sermon about Jesus—the very thing that many young pastors decry as a modern act, when it is in fact simply biblical.

Additionally, church history confirms that from its earliest days, Christianity was marked by megachurches. As early as AD 323, church buildings were reportedly constructed that could accommodate upwards of 10,000 to 20,000 Christian worshipers at a time.[29] Therefore, the existence of larger churches is not a modern phenomenon but is in fact something God has been doing since the days of Pentecost.

In 1980, the largest church in America was 13,000 people, and in 2003, the largest church was 25,000 people.[30] While a church of 25,000 people may seem very large to many, size is indeed relative when you consider the world's largest church, Yoido Full Gospel Church, in Seoul, Korea, which has 763,000 church members.[31] Therefore, each church must ask how large they expect to be and labor toward seeing enough conversions to achieve that goal. In setting this goal, a church must be realistic, since not every church can or should be a megachurch. A church should also not seek to limit its conversion growth simply because they wrongly believe that smaller churches are closer to the early church model.

Question 7

Will your church have a mission of community or be a community of mission?

The buzzword *community* is so often bantered about that it is nearly devoid of meaning. But since the church is a community, it is important to define what kind of community the church should be. Without a clear definition of what a missional church community is and does, tragically, community will become the mission of the church. Consequently, the goal of people will be to hang out together in love, like the family they never had. While this is not evil, it is also not sufficient.

If taken too far, this can lead to the heresy of participatory redemption, in which the goal is to have authentic friendships and a loving community instead of repentance and personal faith in Jesus Christ as the means of salvation. This error is a very real threat that is overlooked by many young Christian leaders I meet who prefer smaller and more loosely defined neo-church arrangements and so-called new monastic communities, in which being in community sometimes takes priority over being in Christ.

In Scripture, we see two prototypical communities: Babel/Babylon and Pentecost. Their similarities and differences are noted below.[32]

Babel Community	Pentecost Community
A small city	A large kingdom
Built to house a few people	Built to house many people
Marked by walls	Marked by no walls
Intentionally resisted diversity	Intentionally pursued diversity
Avoided hospitality	Practiced hospitality
Gathered a homogenous people	Gathered a heterogeneous people
Made their name great	Made Jesus' name great
God came down	God came down
God judged their sin	God forgave their sin
God confused their languages	God unified their languages

The Babylonian version of community is godless affinity. Babylonian community does not aspire to grow except by internal births, does not welcome people who are different, does not practice hospitality, and seeks to remain safe and successful. Community is the only goal for churches who think Babylonian. God's response to Babylonian community is judgment and scattering, because it is a sin, especially in the church.

The Pentecost version of community exists for mission, not for itself. Pentecost community is not held together because people are similar but rather because they are on the same mission with the same Lord. Because of this, Pentecost community is marked by a desire to expand God's kingdom through the salvation of many diverse people, who are hospitably welcomed to learn about the greatness of Jesus. People who think with a Pentecost mindset do not see the building of community in their church as their mission. Rather, they see their church community as existing solely for God's mission, and they accept that the only way to have healthy community is to pursue God's mission of reaching lost people because community is an effect of mission but not an effective mission. God's response to Pentecost missional community is grace and unity through the Holy Spirit.

Question 8

Will your leaders work from guilt or conviction?

One of the greatest inhibitors of keeping a church on mission is the erroneous spoken and unspoken expectations people have for church leaders and their families. In a missional church, the lead pastor is the architect who builds the ship more than he is the captain who pilots it, the cook who washes dishes in the galley, or the activities director who coordinates the shuffleboard reservations.[33] The role of architect is incredibly important because most pastors have been trained how to work on a ship instead of how to build a ship. Having a skilled captain, cook, and activities director is important but does not really matter if the ship can't float, which means that boat building is the most important job. Likewise, the pastor's highest task is to plan the building of a church that will float and to allow everyone else to use their talents and gifts to accomplish the overall mission God has for that church.

Most pastors, however, work in their boat and not on their boat because often the Christians in a pastor's church have mastered the art of making him feel guilty and making their needs seem urgent and important, when they rarely are.[34] Therefore, leaders of emerging and missional churches must work from the conviction that comes from God and his Word instead of from the guilt that comes from people and their words. Leaders must frequently decide between offending Christ or a Christian, and Ghost-guided biblical conviction alone must determine the duties of church leaders. Otherwise, church leaders will waste their time washing dishes while their church sinks.

Question 9

Do you have the guts to shoot your dogs?

Dogs are idiotic ideas, stinky styles, stupid systems, failed facilities, terrible technologies, loser leaders, and pathetic people. Most churches know who and what their dogs are but simply lack the courage to pull the trigger and shoot their dogs. Therefore, it is vital to name with brutal candor the people, programs, structures, and ministry philosophies that are dogs needing to be shot. Be sure to make it count and shoot them only once so that they don't come back and bite you.[35]

Question 10

Can you wield a sword and a trowel?

In the days of Nehemiah, when the Israelites' mission was to rebuild the wall, Nehemiah had his people carry a trowel in one hand to build and a sword in the other to defend their work. As we build our churches in a culture no less hostile than that of Nehemiah, we too must learn how to both build a missional church and defend it from Satan, demons, and evildoers. In the following chapters, I will be painfully honest about the shots from hell that nearly killed my family and our church. In the next chapter, we'll start our journey in the hot upstairs youth room of a fundamentalist church.

Reformission Reflections

1. Do you personally tend toward liberalism, fundamentalism, or reformission? Why?

2. Does your church or ministry tend toward liberalism, fundamentalism, or reformission? Why?

3. Should your church or ministry be traditional, contemporary, or missional? Why?

4. Is your church or ministry better at being attractional or missional? How could improvements be made where it is weak?

5. How large is your church or ministry? How large should it be in the next year, five years, and ten years?

6. Does your church or ministry community exist for the mission of reaching lost people or primarily for itself?

7. Name at least ten dogs in your church or ministry that need to be shot.

8. What does your church or ministry need to be defended from to remain healthy? What can be done to defend it?

CHAPTER ONE

God saved me while I was living with my lesbian mom and my dad was in prison for murder.

I am a founding pastor.

Jesus, Our Offering Was $137 and I Want to Use It to Buy Bullets

0 – 45 People

The upstairs room at the fundamentalist church was so hot that everyone was sweating like Mike Tyson in a spelling bee.[1] During one service, a pregnant lady simply passed out and fell off her chair. This would not have been so traumatic if I were trying to plant one of those shake-and-bake, holy-roller churches where I smacked people on the nugget in Jesus' name so they could lie on the floor and twitch like a freshly caught trout on a dock and call it the work of the Holy Ghost.

It was the first half of 1996 and I was twenty-five years of age chronologically, six years of age spiritually, and trying to gather enough people to launch Mars Hill Church in the city of Seattle. About ten to twenty people a week were showing up for our Sunday service, which had outgrown the living room of my rental home and was now being held in one of those epically awful youth rooms, complete with golden shag carpet on the floor and Christian rock posters on the wall for the poor kids forced to ride the short bus of Christian culture. Our weekly service would start sometime around 6:00 p.m., whenever the college students and indie rockers would show up, because it was apparently very difficult to get up by the crack of dinner. Fortunately, the room was free, which was nearly more than we could afford.

I had spent the previous two years as the college ministry intern plankton at the bottom of the food chain at a multiracial megachurch and had used the youth room to run a college group in Seattle. College ministry soon started to feel like hanging out with an ex-girlfriend, so I hit the eject button because life-stage ministry was a vocational dead end.

What my college students needed was to mentor high school students and hang out with singles who had phased from college into the work world and married couples who had learned what kind of person to be and to marry to make a family work. What they did not need was to hang out with the same immature yahoos they spent all of their time playing "pull my finger" with anyway and going to a free event that was like day care for twenty-one-year-old hormonally enraged porn addicts and video-game aficionados trying to stretch junior high into the retirement years.

So I decided to start a church, for three reasons. First, I hated going to church and wanted one I liked, so I thought I would just start my own. Second, God had spoken to me in one of those weird charismatic moments and told me to start a church. Third, I am scared of God and try to do what he says.

My wife, Grace, and I did not yet have any children, were both working jobs to make ends meet, and spent all our free time changing diapers on our baby church in its infancy phase.[2] Our church was a dysfunctional small group of Christian college kids and chain-smoking indie rockers who all shared the clueless look of a wide-eyed basset hound that just heard a high-pitched whistle.

COACHING CORNER

Infancy is the season of dreaming and envisioning the future, gathering people, raising money, and making plans. The ministry at this stage exists only in the mind of the leader, who seeks to effectively communicate the vision and compel people to help make it a reality. In the infancy phase, the church and the leader are one and the same because the leader is essentially the only person holding the church together and doing most of the work.

In retrospect, our church services were, quite frankly, painful. My preaching was like a combination of boring systematic theology and uninspiring motivational talk from a cranky junior high gym teacher. Our rotating cast of worship leader tryouts ranged from screaming punk rockers—to this day, I have no idea why they were so dramatically depressed—to the kind of happy-clappy Christian praise musicians that you would expect to find playing on a karaoke machine at a Christian homeschool co-op reunion for kids whose moms made their clothes. Our sound system included speakers from a home stereo that were muddy and faint, except when pumping out feedback, of course, since we could not afford real speakers. We used a moody overhead projector for worship that another church had thrown out because it only worked when it felt like it. If I were Hindu, I would guess that the projector was a junior high kid or a union laborer in a former life.

In my imagination, however, I saw an entirely different church, one that did not have a beat-up old couch or a foosball table in the sanctuary. I envisioned a large church that hosted concerts for non-Christian bands and fans on a phat sound system, embraced the arts, trained young men to be godly husbands and fathers, planted other churches, and led people to work with Jesus Christ as missionaries to our city.

Sadly, that church only existed in my mind, and the hard part was figuring out how to get my vision into the minds of other people so that together we could build the church God had put in my imagination. I started to wrestle with some very basic questions that, although I had read widely, I had apparently not connected in a practical way for ministry. These questions continue to drive our ministry so that it remains missional, and I believe they are vitally important for every Christian and Christian leader to continually ask because they keep the person and mission of Jesus as the most important factor in the church and Christian life.[3]

The Missional Ministry Matrix

Priority 1: Christology—Who is Jesus, what has he accomplished, and what has he sent us to do?

Since our little church was meeting in the evening, I spent a lot of time visiting other churches in our area on Sunday mornings to see how things were going, why they were succeeding or failing, and what kinds of people were going to various churches. I can honestly say that visiting many churches was worse than being a vegetarian chef employed at a steak house.

1. Christology

Who is Jesus, what has he accomplished, and what has he sent us to do?

4. Ministry

How does Jesus want me to help serve his mission in our culture through my church?

2. Ecclesiology

How does the Bible tell us to structure our church leadership so that our church can most effectively be God's missionary to our culture?

3. Missiology

How can we most effectively expand God's kingdom where we are sent?

What kept nagging me about each church I visited was that no matter what the tradition or theological persuasion was, they generally had a crooked Christology. What I mean is this: in visiting numerous churches scattered across the city and throughout the surrounding suburbs, rarely did I hear a clear declaration of the person of Jesus Christ. He was never presented as the eternal God who incarnated as a man in culture to live without sin, die as a substitute for sinners, and resurrect in triumphant victory over Satan, sin, and death; who is now exalted as King of Kings and Lord of Lords; and who is coming again to judge the living and the dead, sending the repentant to his heavenly kingdom and sentencing the unrepentant to his fiery hell.

In the more mainline liberal churches, I heard about the halo-diaper Christ. He was presented as little more than a marginalized Galilean peasant who took a beating as an example for the little guys of the world who get pushed around by bullies and cry a lot. In the more mainstream evangelical churches, Jesus was presented as a sort of buddy Christ, who was a motivational life coach who could help you lose weight and make more money with his pithy acronyms and cheerleader enthusiasm.

In both cases, Jesus was shown only in the selective partial portrait that best suited the agenda of the church, which ranged from gay rights to environmentalism, financial prosperity, and emotional euphoria, depending on the church. What I did not witness was an understanding of exactly who Jesus was and is and what he had accomplished through his incarnation, death, resurrection, and exaltation.

It was not so much that the various churches were wrong per se but that they were incomplete in their selective presentations of Jesus. In the more modern churches, the triumph of the resurrected Jesus was stressed to emphasize victory, so that being a Christian basically meant you were on the winning team with Jesus and, therefore, you were a real winner. What they overlooked was the incarnation of Jesus. Simply, they ignored the fact that Jesus humbly entered into culture to identify with and effectively reach lost people steeped in various kinds of sin. This oversight allowed people to triumphantly parade their victory over sin and sinners but failed to call them to humbly incarnate as missionaries in culture to effectively reach lost people. Christians with this mindset can easily come to see themselves as winners and lost people as losers and consequently are often despised by lost people, who find them smug.

Conversely, many other churches more akin to the so-called postmodern churches focused almost exclusively on vegetable-munching hippie Christ's humble incarnation in culture to hang out with sinful lost people, particularly the poor and marginalized. In this mindset, being a Christian means being a nice person who loves people no matter what their lives are like by trying to identify with their cultural experiences and perspectives in a nonjudgmental and empathetic manner. What is lacking, however, is the understanding that when we next see Jesus, he will not appear as a humble, marginalized Galilean peasant. Rather, we will see the exalted, tattooed King of Kings coming with fire blazing in his eyes and a sword launching from his mouth, with which to make war upon the unrepentant. Until the day of Jesus' second coming, we are not merely to relate to people but also to command them to repent of sin and bend their knee to the King before they are grapes crushed under his foot in the winepress of his fury.

We need both portraits, the humble, incarnated Christ and the triumphant, exalted Christ, to truly understand Jesus Christ. As we get to know the humble, incarnated Christ, we learn how to be missional and lovingly relate to people in their culture. As we get to know the glorified, exalted Christ, we learn to be confident and bold because we proclaim his victory over Satan, sin, death, and hell.

It took a lot of hours reading my Bible, especially the incarnational gospel of John and the exaltational Revelation of John, to sort this out in my mind theologically. In the end, I realized that we labor *with* the exalted Christ, which gives us authority to proclaim the gospel of freedom. And we labor *like* the incarnated Christ, which gives us humility and grace to creatively demonstrate and proclaim the love of Christ to fellow sinners in our culture. And though I needed to be like Jesus and lead our people in kind, I also needed to remember that there is one way in which a Christian should not be like Jesus. Jesus never sinned and, therefore, never repented, but because we sin, we must continually repent if we are to be faithful missionaries. This simple point is important because, while the many emerging pastors I speak with have rightly focused on following the example of Jesus, if they fail to recognize this vital difference between us and Jesus, they will diminish the acknowledgment of sin and the urgency of repentance.

The more I read the Bible, the more deeply the Holy Spirit convicted me that I had grievously erred by trying to figure out how to do church successfully by reading a lot of books, visiting a lot of churches, and copying whatever was working. Instead, I needed to first wrestle with Jesus like Jacob wrestled with Jesus and then discover what Jesus' mission was for Seattle and repent of everything I thought and did that was not congruent with his mission for our city. Only then could I faithfully lead our church to follow our Senior Pastor, Jesus, on his mission in our culture, with the humility of his incarnation and the strength of his exaltation.

Priority 2: Ecclesiology — How does the Bible tell us to structure our church leadership so that our church can most effectively be God's missionary to our culture?

Before God rebuked me, my primary mission was to get a lot of people to show up on Sundays to listen to me preach. But once I realized that the mission of the church was not simply to see how many people would come to listen to my pithy insights, I saw that I had to spread the workload so that we could scatter for mission and not just gather for Mark.

Even though our church was no bigger than some Mormon families, it was wearing me out. Like most pastors of small churches, I was doing a lot of deacon work. I would unlock the building, photocopy my sermon notes, help set up our cutting-edge Fisher Price sound system, set up chairs, welcome visitors, hand out the sermon notes, run the service, and clean up the room when everyone left. During the week, I would answer the phone, answer email, go through the mail, and do whatever else needed to be done, including driving around frantically before the service to pick people up.

Thankfully, a handful of faithful servants picked up the slack, so the church was more than just one highly motivated young guy without any real skills in management. I learned that in a small church, ministry is generally something the pastor does for his people and that the people chip in if and when they feel like it. I feared that if this mindset remained in my church, it would either fail to grow or grow and bury me in work for lazy and ungrateful church people.

As our church continued to meet, it became clear that three basic types of people were showing up. Observers were happy to do and give nothing but just came to watch the show each week, not unlike the people who hit the brakes when driving past a nasty car wreck to gaze and grin. Consumers likewise gave and did nothing but were always wanting more and making demands for more goods and services from me. Participants were the handful of people who had bought into the idea of the church being a missionary to our city. They came to church seeking a way to serve a greater mission and were enormously encouraging.

I soon tried to spend most of my time with the participants in our mission rather than with the observers or consumers of our church. I continually repeated our mission each Sunday from the pulpit—to honor God through the gospel as a church transforming the city—so that the people who stayed in the church understood that they were not welcome to bring any other agenda. The problem was that many of the people who came to the church had been sucking the life out of various program-driven, seeker-sensitive churches for years and ended up being basically worthless for mission. Week after week, they would walk in to see that we did not have the program they wanted and then walk back out, never thinking that perhaps they should serve Christ and build a ministry.

The college kids and singles who had sucked resources from youth groups and parachurch ministries for their entire life without serving or giving were generally just more dead weight to drag around. The young arty types were more willing to serve, providing it was something cool and up-front like playing worship music or speaking to the group in eccentric bohemian fashion, which would be tough to organize because if they all were on the stage, we'd have no one else left to sit in the room and watch them be cool.

In retrospect, I made some very strategic errors that nearly killed the progress of our church. First, I had a very informal leadership structure, as is common in small churches, which permitted heretics, nutjobs, and pushy types to wield a lot of power. Worse still, it was hard to know how to remove such people without killing the church since it was so small that we were one social network and to remove one person was to risk losing every person.

Second, the church was based on relationships that were all connected to me, and we did not have formal small groups to connect people to each other. This kept me from working on growing the church, and I got stuck being friends with the handful of people we already had. This became particularly obvious when my truck and I seemed to be moving every college student in the church each school year.

Third, I had not clearly articulated in written form what we would and would not fight over theologically, which led to some tremendous problems and got us branded as a cult by some outsiders. I also did not explain in written form that we were theologically conservative and culturally liberal, which caused great confusion because half of the church was angry that the other half was smoking, while the other half was angry that I taught from the Bible.

Fourth, I greatly underestimated Solomon's statement that "money is the answer for everything" (Eccl. 10:19). Somehow I got the idea that money was a dirty thing and that to talk about it, receive it, or spend it was also dirty. To this day, I am not sure where this silly idea came from, but I was willing to have both my wife and I work full-time to pay the bills for our little church, to the point that she began having stress-related health problems. I raised outside support to cover part of a salary so that I could work for the church for free and left a box in the back corner of the room on Sundays, telling people that if God led them to give, they could. Apparently, the Ghost only led people to give once every presidential election, and I hit rock bottom one Sunday when our offering was $137. I stood alone in the room, counting the money and cussing at the offering box for being filled with one-dollar bills and the ominous smell of imminent death. Obviously, I had to quickly figure out how to organize our church with real elders, real deacons, and real Christians so that we could get to our mission of reaching lost people.

At the time, it was becoming increasingly popular for young pastors to have churches that were not called "churches" but rather silly things like "new monastic communities" and leaders that were not called "pastor" but rather silly things like "abbess" or "spiritual director." As our mission began to develop, the New Testament teaching on church leadership and church discipline seemed increasingly wise and urgent to implement, before we ended up like the church at Corinth, divided and off mission because of folly and sin. Over the years, I have become increasingly troubled by the frequency with which young pastors simply dismiss the New Testament teaching on church leadership and discipline, so that if four guys are drinking beer in a pub, they can call it a church. One well-known expert promoting this new undefined, undisciplined, and unbiblical ecclesiology was once asked how we can possibly define what a church is if his advice of not having elders, deacons, members, discipline, or doctrine was heeded. His response was simply, "If it smells like a church, it is a church." My response was that sometimes a whore wears the same perfume as a wife, and it's no different with the bride of Christ.

God deeply burdened me to thoroughly study and submit to the biblical teaching on church leadership. People's eternal lives were at stake, and I would one day stand before Jesus to give an account for each person that he had entrusted to me to pastor, leaving no room for ecclesiological experimentation or for vainly creating new definitions of church because I wanted to be cool (Heb. 13:17).[4] Pastors who want to do mission need to first meet the New Testament requirements of an elder-pastor and then train other men to be qualified pastors and men and women to be qualified deacons. Without biblical leadership, mission cannot happen because no one has the authority to define the mission, direct the mission, or defend the mission. This explains why church ecclesiology was so important to Paul, who followed Jesus' example of appointing men to the highest positions of spiritual leadership. When biblical church leadership is in place, people can be more effectively trained for ministry that is meaningful because it is missional.

Priority 3: Missiology—How can we most effectively expand God's kingdom where we are sent?

While visiting the various church services in proximity to our church, it struck me as curious that although all the congregations claimed to be Christian, they were clearly all on very different missions. One church was particularly confusing. They promoted homosexuality but made me take off my ball cap upon entering the church. It seemed odd that a male greeter who had likely had sex with a man before church chastised me for wearing a hat in church because I was disrespecting God.

The woman pastor of this church, wearing a very nice, flowing, cutting-edge-of-1536 robe, talked about rainbows for twenty minutes while sixty or so very old people who were former classmates of Noah and eyewitnesses to the covenant rainbow sat scattered among one thousand seats or so and napped in Jesus' name. Between her sermonette, the written literature I picked up that told me how to bequeath my estate to the church when I die, and looking around the room at the equivalent of a Viagra before-photo of lifeless geriatrics, I truly could not discern why that church existed. The closest I came to finding someone with a mission was the children's pastor, namely the meek husband of the senior pastor in pumps, who said his goal was to make his wife happy, which made me very sad.

Down the street, another woman pastor and her gay male associate pastor with a lovely rainbow on his elegantly sassy robe both spoke passionately about the need to get rid of our nuclear weapons. Their message did not connect with me because I did not have any nuclear weapons. So I left early.

At a church in the suburbs, I was impressed with their very cool building but a bit bummed that the church web address was the same as the pastor's name, because it seemed a bit pretentious, like rapper P Diddy a.k.a. Sean John, who wears his own clothing line with his name emblazoned on the front of his shirt. Conversely, I was also a little jealous because it did sound a bit cool to have a church named after me, complete with my photo on the side of buses so that everyone would know that I was pastor izzle fo' shizzle. From the printed material and the sermon, it was readily apparent that this church was into the bling Christ, who will make you rich and cure all your diseases, except for the epidemics of consumerism and eighties charismullet hair, of course. They even taught that Jesus was a rich man and that only people who lack faith get sick, presumably like the junior varsity Job and Paul. For them, Jesus was a piñata, Christianity was a whacking stick, and their mission was to teach people how to get goodies to fall out of heaven.

One fundamentalist church I visited was doing a series on Revelation, and the pastor's face was so red that I thought he was going to blow a gasket. He yelled about the end of the world at the battle of Armageddon, which was going to happen in ten or fifteen minutes, from what I could surmise. Unlike the pastor of the liberal church, this dude was a full-blown, big-gutted, heterosexual, gun-shooting, truck-driving, meat-eating, fire-and-brimstone-preaching Bible thumper from the old school. He was my favorite, even though he used the King James Version and said homosexual like it was three words, "ho-mo-sexual."

His point was that Satan had taken over the media with the help of the Jews and that some secret group of government leaders with a really scary name like Illuminati were meeting behind closed doors to usher in a one-world government. Presumably, it would be led by none other than the Antichrist, who would make us all get bar codes on our heads so we could be scanned like jars of mayonnaise at the grocery story and run through a wood chipper if we did not pray to Satan and eat our children. Fortunately, the pastor told us about the rapture and how, if we don't watch television and do vote Republican, we can fly to heaven just before Jesus opens a can of whoop in the end. This man was on a mission, but it wasn't very missional. His mission seemed to be simply to get off the planet as soon as possible, which didn't sound very incarnational to me.

I visited a lot of other churches, but you get the point. No matter what the tradition or theological perspective, the one common thread that wove all of the churches together was that they were each on their own mission instead of on Jesus' mission to transform people and cultures by the power of the Holy Spirit through the work of the gospel. And each church conveniently grabbed the snapshot of Jesus that best suited their mission and used it to legitimize and bless their mission in his name. Theologically, this was profoundly troubling, because I was certain that Jesus was on his own mission and that any church not on that mission had what Paul called another gospel and another Jesus, concocted by a cunning Serpent.

During this time, I was deeply convicted that until this point I too had been on my own mission with my church, trying to reach hip postmodern people and have hip music and basically just do the cool church thing. I had grown facial hair, started cussing again (I had stopped for about fifteen minutes after I got saved), and briefly considered taking up smoking but had asthma, which kept me from achieving my full cool potential. But I was certain that while Jesus did not mind if hip postmoderns got saved or if our band was rockin' like Dokken, he did have bigger things in mind when he got out of his tomb on Easter Sunday than me growing facial hair, cussing, and rocking out. This led me to consider the next question: What exactly had Jesus assigned to our church as our part in his mission in our city? To learn the answer, I obviously needed more time in prayer and Scripture to listen to what God would say.

Priority 4: Ministry—How does Jesus want me to help serve his mission in our culture through my church?

I know this may sound nuts, but when you are the only pastor on staff at a small church, you don't have a boss, a job description, or a general clue what you are supposed to be doing. In some ways, I felt like the kid in that movie *Home Alone.*

Trying to figure out what I was supposed to be doing, I met with a few other pastors to inquire about their typical day. I learned that small church pastors go out to lunch a lot, answer the phone, counsel people, tidy up the church building, labor to put together a mediocre sermon, and sit in their offices looking sacred so that if people drop by, they feel like they are getting their money's worth from their pastor.

Since my office was in our home, we were borrowing the youth room at the fundamentalist church on Sundays, and I did not like to counsel people, I decided that I would just do what I believed Jesus wanted of me after spending hours studying the epistles and praying for direction. I did not want to be an employee of the church, keeping shop by working for church people, much like a hotel concierge sitting by a desk, waiting for the phone to ring so that customers can be well served no matter what their outrageous demands are. Believing I worked for Jesus and not the church, I decided to spend my time with Jesus, prayerfully investigating the city like a missionary, trying to figure out what Jesus' mission was for our city. Over the years, I have accepted that I'm really not much of a pastor but rather am a missiologist studying the city who leads a church filled with missionaries who reach the city and with pastors who care for the converts.

I tried to figure out why the different neighborhoods in our city functioned as tribes that shared values and experiences. I hung out on college campuses, observing students and asking them about their spirituality, and killed time in various bars, coffee shops, and restaurants, observing people to determine why they were drawn to these places instead of to local churches. I met with people who were shaping our culture, such as real estate brokers, chamber of commerce members, business leaders, musicians, and basically anyone who would talk to me. I also spent time hanging out with the homeless kids who loitered near the university, trying to figure out what their family systems had been like. This was a season of listening, since I was not actively trying to save anyone just yet but rather trying first to understand them so that I could build a church best suited to reach people like them and to change the culture that contributed to their problems.

But to make that happen, I had to focus all of my time and energy on growing Mars Hill as a missional church for Seattle. Therefore, I had to stop doing all other ministry work that was not accomplishing this objective. As you can imagine, this presented me with difficult decisions. At the time, I was cohosting a national radio show called *Street Talk*, founded by a dear friend named Lief Moi. We spent Saturday nights from 9:00 p.m. to midnight answering spiritual questions from the usual bag of mixed nuts listening to the radio while driving home drunk.

The show itself was a bit of a miracle. We had no sponsors, no real budget, and no paid staff. On a whim, Lief raised enough money through one of those chicken-dinner fundraisers to get our local show beamed up to a broadcast satellite. But no market in the country agreed to pick us up. One night we unexpectedly started getting calls from the great nation of Texas because the board operator at a radio station forgot to turn off the satellite feed. The listeners liked the show enough to call the station and plead for our show to remain on air, and that is how we got into our first national market. The miracles continued until we were on some thirty stations across the country.

I really enjoyed the show because it was successful in bringing the gospel to a wide audience and taught me a lot about the thoughts and questions of lost people. I needed to quit the show at this point, however, to focus on our struggling little church. Lief later shut the radio show down altogether, though it was successful, to also focus on our church. I also killed the small college ministry that I had started, and most of those students scattered like chaff in the wind, though a handful jumped on board to help start the church.

Speaking to other pastors, I learned that many pastors, particularly pastors of small churches, are busy but bored like I was. They spend their time taking care of their people and running services but don't have much of a mission to keep their pilot light lit. So they tend to volunteer time in other ministries, such as overseas missions trips, parachurch organizations, and the like, to do something more than just answer the phone and meet with the same handful of people that already know Christ and drive the pastors nuts. I was convicted that rather than spending my time supporting auxiliary ministries outside of our church, I should labor to build a church that would satisfy my ministry desires by being on mission with Jesus to transform my city by the power of the gospel. To do this, I would need to stay doggedly focused on our mission. Over the years, this has become increasingly difficult because the other pastors in our area, whom I do sincerely love, are prone to jump on various bandwagons, from political causes to social agendas, and want me to do the same. I refuse to join them not because they are wrong but because their projects are off my God-given mission and, therefore, are a waste of my time and energy, not unlike a hockey player spending hours perfecting his curveball.

So in an effort to clarify our mission, I wrote down on paper the first of what would eventually be many strategic plans. I shot for the moon rather foolishly and decided that our church that was not big enough to fill a bus would plant multiple churches, run a concert venue, start a Bible institute, write books, host conferences, and change the city for Jesus. I started handing out these goals printed on boring white paper without any graphics, colors, or cool fonts, naively assuming that it would all happen eventually because it was what Jesus wanted.

To get leaders in place for world domination, I also spent time trying to articulate the vision in my head to good men who would be qualified to rise up as fellow elders-pastors. So, as Jesus did, I spent time in prayer asking the Father which of his sons should be trained for leadership. The church started as an idea I shared with Lief Moi and Mike Gunn. Lief is a descendant of Genghis Khan and his dad was a murderer, and Mike is a former football player. They proved to be invaluable, except for the occasional moments when they would stand toe-to-toe in a leadership meeting, threatening to beat the Holy Spirit out of each other. Both men were older than I and had years of ministry experience, and they were good fathers, loving husbands, and tough. Too often this last point is overlooked, but when Paul said that a pastor must fight like a soldier, train like an athlete, and work hard like a farmer, he had in mind the manliest of men leading the church (2 Tim. 2:1–7). Sadly, the weakest men are often drawn to ministry simply because it is an indoor job that does not require heavy lifting.

To prepare the best men that I had to become pastors-elders, we started meeting with Eric Brown, who is currently on staff at Imago Dei Church in Portland (part of our Acts 29 Network), Campus Crusade for Christ staff member Chris Knutzen, and a man named Kirk Schlemlein. All of us were converted later in life, which was helpful because we were focused on reaching lost people and could relate to lost people. In time, this group became the official elder council and ruled the church through some incredibly tough seasons. The key was that each man was a player who could do ministry and a coach who could train other leaders. Since we were flat broke with no staff, I needed a team of player-coaches who could get things done and lead the church through the sheer force of their godly influence.

Our church was so small that I knew everyone by name and visitors stuck out like strangers at a family reunion. For reasons that are still unclear to me, people started visiting our little neo-Amish, punk-rock enclave, maybe just because it was new and there was a buzz about a new kind of church. The good news was that I was the pastor of a growing church. The bad news was that I was a bad pastor of a bad church and had a lot of mistakes to undo.

Reformission Reflections

1. Does your church or ministry have a clear biblical understanding of Jesus? If not, what else do your people need to learn?

2. Is your church or ministry led by qualified and respected leaders? What can you do to support the leaders in your church?

3. Articulate in one sentence the mission Jesus has called your church or ministry to. Would the people in your church or ministry give the same answer, or are there contradictory missions and confusion in your church or ministry? What can be done to bring people who are not on mission in line with the mission?

4. What ministry are you currently doing to help serve Jesus' mission in your culture through your church? What are you learning as you serve?

CHAPTER TWO

We were the first family at the church and today our dad is a pastor.

Jesus, If Anyone Else Calls My House, I May Be Seeing You Real Soon

45 – 75 People

As I held the knife in my hand, my chest puffed out in pride. I knew in the depths of my soul that I had finally become a man. I can still remember that life-changing day when I was asked to leave the kids' table and told to sit instead at the adults' table for Thanksgiving dinner. Unlike the kids' table, the adults' table had cups without lids, dangerous knives for cutting your own food, and a curious absence of mashed potatoes being flicked between warring diners.

Likewise, I was proud when our childish church eventually outgrew the stinky, hot upstairs youth room at the fundamentalist church. Subsequently, our mighty nation of some forty-five assorted mixed nuts moved into the sanctuary of the church, which felt like we had metaphorically left the kids' table in favor of the adults' table.

It was the middle of 1996, and we continued meeting at 6:00 p.m. because we could not find a place to have services on Sunday mornings. Renting the sanctuary cost $1,000 a month, which was a great deal of money at the time because we were struggling to just get up to broke. I occasionally bought lottery tickets and promised God I would tithe if he'd let me win, but to no avail. We decided to go ahead and rent the sanctuary anyway because we wanted more seats so that we could reach more people and had faith that God would bring in the money because we were on his mission.

I was feeling a bit abused and disrespected by our church, not unlike a babysitter for a legion of Rosemary's babies. But one day, totally out of the blue, a guy named Pete called me "Pastor," something no one had ever done before. I felt like I was finally getting some respect — until Pete laughed and punched me in the shoulder, saying he was only kidding. I wanted to give him the metaphorical right hand of fellowship but chose to just walk away. In retrospect, this disrespect may also have had something to do with the fact that I often preached in a ball cap and said "dude" and "bro" a lot.

The church office was still in our home, which was odd. I spent my days getting up, getting dressed, and sitting in my living room by myself, pretending to have office hours, which proved unproductive. Occasionally someone would call, but being a heterosexual man who hates to talk on the phone, I soon got sick of answering it. I also quickly learned that if I answered the phone, the same people would call more frequently, and I did not really want to talk to them because they were a lot like Bill Murray's character in the movie *What about Bob?*

This was drilled home for me one night when the church phone in our house rang at some godforsaken hour when I'm not even a Christian, like 3:00 a.m. I answered it in a stupor, and on the other line was some college guy who was crying. I asked him what was wrong, and he said it was an emergency and he really needed to talk to me. Trying to muster up my inner pastor, I sat down and tried to pretend I was concerned. I asked him what was wrong, and he rambled for a while about nothing, which usually means that a guy has sinned and is wasting time with dumb chitchat because he's ashamed to just get to the point and confess. So I interrupted him blurting out, "It's three a.m., so stop jerking me around. What have you done?"

"I masturbated," he said.

"That's it?" I said.

"Yes," he replied. "Tonight I watched a porno and I masturbated."

"Is the porno over?" I asked.

"Yes," he said.

"Was it a good porno?" I asked.

He did not reply.

"Well, you've already watched the whole porno and tugged your tool, so what am I supposed to do?" I asked.

"I don't know," he said. "You are my pastor, so I thought that maybe you could pray for me."

To be honest, I did not want to pray, so I just said the first thing that came to mind. "Jesus, thank you for not killing him for being a pervert. Amen," I prayed.

"Alright, well you should sleep good now, so go to bed and don't call me again tonight because I'm sleeping and you are making me angry," I said.

"Well, what I am supposed to do now?" he asked.

"You need to stop watching porno and crying like a baby afterward and grow up, man. I don't have time to be your accountability partner, so you need to be a man and nut up and take care of this yourself. A naked lady is good to look at, so get a job, get a wife, ask her to get naked, and look at her instead. Alright?" I said.

"Alright. Thanks, Pastor Mark," he said as I hung up the phone and walked back to bed shaking my head.

He actually called me "Pastor" and was not laughing like Pete had, which was an encouraging first. You may think I'm a jerk of a counselor, but I think deep down most other pastors think like I do and just don't say what they think because they lack whatever deep psychological problem I have that prevents me from filtering my words through a grid of propriety. The truth is that the guy actually did what I told him and today has a wife and some kids and no longer watches porno.

The next day I sat alone in my house, wondering if I really wanted to be a pastor. Meanwhile, the phone kept ringing. So I turned the ringer off because it was otherwise very hard to ignore.

I decided that though a pastor was supposed to answer the phone and help people, I would end up with a gun to my head if I did. And since I had no boss and the church was not paying me, I decided to just keep doing what I thought Jesus wanted me to do instead of doing what the people in the church wanted me to do. I realized that people would not be knocking on my door asking me to save them or be their pastor, so I decided to just go get some more people and let my other leaders deal with the ones we already had. For me, our church was not the people we had but primarily the people we did not yet have, and I needed to go get those people. I'm still not sure if most pastors are aware that their churches are comprised of people they don't yet know. Those people will never come to the churches, so the pastors need to go to those people.

The hard part was figuring out where to begin in trying to gather people. It seemed weird to just start hitting on total strangers at places like coffee shops, trying to get them to pray the sinner's prayer, like a spiritual flasher.

After a few days of leaving the ringer off, I felt guilty and turned the phone back on. But the phone started ringing again and I could not concentrate, so I ignored the phone and went for a walk to prayerfully think through how I could meet people to bring them to our church.

Then it dawned on me that we were getting a visitor or two at church every week and that low-hanging fruit would probably be the easiest to pick. So on Sundays I started carrying a stack of blank notecards in my pocket. Our church was small enough that I knew who the visitors were. I would walk up, introduce myself, and ask a few leading questions to see if they were members at another church or visiting from out of town because I did not want to waste my time. Those people who seemed worth getting to know would get a card on which to write down their contact information, and I would schedule a meeting with them on the spot and write it in my appointment book to ensure we had a scheduled appointment.

I started by scheduling meetings in coffee shops because I had no office and no money to pay for lunch. Worse still, I wasn't even a coffee drinker. I spent the weekdays driving all over the region to meet with people and tell them the gospel and sell them on my mission for our church. Some of the time I got stood up after driving more than an hour to a meeting, so I started bringing books to read while I waited. But I kept scheduling meetings in an effort to convert the lost to Jesus and convert the found to our mission with Jesus so that the church could move forward. I soon noticed that those people I had personally connected with tended to stick with our church, start serving, and start bringing friends to church who I would then meet with over coffee to repeat the cycle. It actually worked, and, one person at a time, we slowly began to grow.

Our church services started to stink a whole lot less. We scraped together enough money to buy some big honking speakers, and I stole an unused sound console from my old church along with a projection screen, which were sins that Jesus thankfully died to forgive. After a series of incredibly painful worship leader auditions, not unlike the reject episodes of *American Idol*, we finally landed a guy who was a legitimately good worship leader. But then his wife ran off on him and he needed a break, so we returned to stinking again. It felt like finally getting a date with the hot girl only to have her dump you on the first date right after a good kiss.

At this point, we were running between fifty and sixty young people. Then we finally got some older people who came two Sundays in a row, which was a big deal. I introduced myself and discovered that they were Brethren people. I did not know what a Brethren person was but did notice that they carried King James Bibles, Mom had a doily on her head, and Dad wanted to argue about the rapture a lot. Their huge pile of kids all shared the glazed look of lobotomy test cases. From what I could tell, their father actually had a job, which meant he might tithe, and no one in their family had been in rehab before, so it seemed like we were on the brink of becoming more cross-cultural.

I asked them if they were interested in committing to the church, and they said that their only requirement was that their kids could perform their handbell choir routine in front of the church on Sundays. Honestly, I did not know what a handbell choir was, and they tried to explain it, but I did not understand. So the following Sunday the kids brought their handbells to church to give me a demonstration. The mom beamed under her doily as the kids put on their white gloves and started banging their bells in what I guess is what you consider a lovely song if your dad is not a construction worker who drives an El Camino, like my dad.

When the kids finished, I tried to explain that I did not think that white gloves and handbells would be popular with our chain-smoking indie rockers. The Brethren people said they would be willing to allow the indie rockers to play worship music first as long as their kids could do their handbell choir performance at the end of the church services as a sort of grand finale.

It was at that time that I realized our church would never have a sign out front that said "Everyone welcome," because I did not want everyone. Instead, I wanted people who would reach out to the lost young people in our area. So the Brethren folks and their handbells and their doily left our church.

Around the same time, we had a very peculiar thing happen. We had avowed to be nothing but a church for college students and singles. Though we did not run a nursery or accommodate families with young children, another family with young children showed up. They were so old they seemed downright antediluvian. Phil and Jen were in their thirties, really nice people, spiritually mature, did not own an electric guitar, did not smoke, did not have tattoos, and did not ask for anything. They did say that they felt called to help our church by serving in any way we needed and giving money. They were actually serious about wanting to stick with us.

Phil asked what our plan was for child care, and I told him we did not do anything for children. He kindly asked if I had any children, and I said no. He then asked if I intended to have any kids, and I said yes. He then asked what I planned to do with my kids. And I had no idea. So we were on the horns of a terrible dilemma. I had foolishly told our church that we would not do anything for kids, but it became obvious that eventually almost everyone in the church would get married and have kids, and some would also have kids before they were married because they were sinfully fornicating. Either way, we needed to have a plan for kids.

A buzz was growing about ministry to Generation X. In retrospect, this was a dumb idea, which should have been obvious because the name "Generation X" was made up by a Canadian guy. Worse still, he probably ripped off the name from the Billy Idol song of the same name. Anyway, I declared that we would be a Generation X church because it seemed cool. To this day I cannot fathom why I was so stupid, because I obviously was not going to card people at the door like a bar to make sure they were born between certain years to attend our church and hear the gospel. Within a few months of study on the issue, I came to a number of conclusions about generational age-specific ministry that made me regret declaring such a dumb thing.

First, the fat old white guys from the Midwest with more degrees than Fahrenheit who were writing books on Generation X knew as much about Generation X as a redneck does about Dostoyevsky. They were all saying that those people born between roughly 1965 and 1976 would be the poorest generation in history, starving to death and wandering around naked and gaunt like a nation of supermodels. But the people in my church were starting small, profitable tech companies and digging into the Internet pot of gold at Microsoft.

Second, as I studied Scripture, I learned that a generation refers to the people living on the earth at a particular time and not to various age groups (e.g., Num. 32:13; Matt. 17:17). So the Bible was not interested in focusing on people between certain birthdays but rather in bringing the gospel to everyone who is breathing, because those are the kind of people God has called us to reach. Therefore, not only was having a church that catered only to people between certain ages narrow, it was also sinful because God loves the whole world and not just white guys between their teens and late twenties.

Third, as I studied the history of pop culture, I learned that the generational theory was a recent invention that apparently began with the hippies. The story is that the hippies were the first American generation to break from their parents and forge for themselves an independent identity marked by getting stoned more than the apostle Paul and raging against some guy called "the man," who was apparently quite busy causing every evil in the world. As I researched the hippies, I learned that the Christian version of being hippiefied was called the Jesus Movement and led to such nondenominational denominations as Calvary Chapel and the Vineyard.

Since a lot of the people in my church played guitar and sinfully smoked pot, I thought that maybe the hippie pastors could help me figure out what to do. So I went to some of their churches. Sadly, all the hippie Christians I met had become yuppies who stopped raging against "the man" so that they could get haircuts, minivans, and become "the man." This further confirmed that generational identity is very faddish and that eventually people sober up, get a job, get married, pump out a few kids, fall into a predictable rut of voting Republican to lower their taxes, and graduate from homegrown pot to prescription medication to manage their unspectacular life under the sun.

Fourth, after reading more books and articles than I cared to, I decided to just start asking some of the new converts who had met Christ in our church what would most help them to grow in their relationship with Jesus. Each young person I spoke to said they wanted to be connected to people younger and older than themselves. The young urban arty types God had burdened me to build a church for generally came from jacked-up homes, which they wanted to overcome in hopes of one day having a decent future for themselves and their kids. But they had no idea what a decent Christian family looked like. So what they needed was a friendship with godly older families to learn about marriage and parenting. The last thing they needed was a mono-generational church.

The only problem was that our city has less Christians and young children than nearly every other city in our nation.[1] Tragically, we actually have less children than dogs in our city.[2] And finding godly older families who were willing to serve new converts instead of demanding to fill their face at our programming trough proved tougher than finding someone with an IQ bigger than their waist working at the Department of Motor Vehicles.

So I decided we needed to welcome Phil, Jen, and their kids as a gift from God. We also needed to make our church accommodating to other families, not simply to attract consumers but to welcome families who wanted to be missionaries, opening their homes and sharing their lives with lost people and new converts to give them a picture of what the gospel does to transform lives.

That Sunday, I repented before our church for my dumb idea of having a Generation X church, which was good because it set the precedent of me standing up to recant my dumb ideas so that we can get unstuck on our mission of bringing the gospel of Jesus to our city. So we started running a nursery for small children during our service. Curiously, the singles and college students really enjoyed getting to know children and their families and began volunteering to play with the kids. It dawned on me that by working with the kids, a lot of our young people were learning from the kids about parenting and were learning from friendships with the parents what kind of person they would need to become to marry and begin a family of their own.

Young couples also started falling in love and wanted to get married. So I wrote a series of premarital Bible studies. Before long, this became a quarterly Bible study that filled our home to capacity because little biblical teaching on gender, marriage, and family was available in our city. We encouraged the young couples to send us their friends who were approaching marriage, which helped our church grow.

Eventually I'll write some books on these subjects, but for the sake of brevity, I will now simply come out of the closet and reveal that I am an intense biblical literalist who believes that the man is the head of the home, that the man should provide for his family, that children are a blessing, and that we would not have so many deceived feminists running around if men were better husbands and fathers because the natural reaction of godly women to godly men is trust and respect. For some, this theological instruction was as popular as a fart in an elevator, and they left our church. But the more than one hundred couples we trained in the first few years of the class remain happily married today and serve Jesus as missionaries, knowing that their marriage is for the gospel as much as the gospel is for their marriage.

So I had to buy my first suit and figure out how to officiate a wedding. In time, I got pretty comfortable doing the gig and had a lot of fun seeing people marry. The most enjoyable weddings were those of couples who came to faith in Jesus during the premarital Bible study in our home.

The couples who did premarital counseling with us caught our vision for the church and became some of our best and most devoted church leaders. They started doing a lot of ministry without being asked or organized and simply started taking matters into their own hands. Before long, we had people opening their homes to host Bible studies, various house parties on weekends, baby showers for expecting moms, and wedding showers for new brides, and also delivering meals to new moms recovering from birth and showing up early and staying late on Sundays to help get things done for the service.

Though our church was still small, I was surprised at how quickly I became buried in caring for only a few people. Because I was a brand-new pastor, I learned to provide pastoral care on the job, which is a lot like taking a driver's education class by driving a stick shift on the freeway during rush hour. For example, one young man who was a newer Christian engaged to be married called me late one night and asked me to hurry to the hospital. When I got there, he informed me that his only living relative, his mother, had doused herself in gasoline and lit herself on fire in an attempt to commit suicide. She had burned her entire body, was lying near death in the hospital, and was being kept alive by a machine. He did not know if he should pull the plug and let her die or try to keep her alive despite the fact that she was as good as dead. I had no idea what to say. On one hand, it seemed the woman clearly wanted to die, and the doctors said she would die but it could be weeks or months of lingering pain before that happened. On the other hand, the young man did not want to live with the guilt of causing the death of his own mother. I remember sitting in the hospital lobby with my face in my hands, praying James 1:5 over and over. To make matters worse, his mother was not saved, in a coma, and likely brain-dead, which prevented us from sharing the gospel with her. In the end, we decided to pull the plug, and he watched his unsaved mother die quickly.

Emotionally, ministry proved to be more exhausting than I could have fathomed. Because I deeply loved my people and carried their burdens, the pains of our people's lives began to take a deep toll on me. Many nights were spent in prayer for people instead of sleeping, and even on what were supposed to be days off, my mind was consumed with the painful hardships and sinful rebellions of our people.

By this time, a bit of a buzz was going out about our church, but no one could find us because we had no office from which to coordinate communication and we were meeting in a rented church on Sunday nights. A friend in the church named Marc was a tech guy and put together a website without even being asked. Since it was pretty dang cool, I gave him permission to put it on the Internet, and it really did help people find us and made a statement to the young tech crowd that we shared their value for technology. Curiously, our website quickly became our new front door through which people passed before they showed up at church.

And we finally landed a good worship leader. Brad was a godly guy with a nice wife, who fronted a local band that was big in the club-scene heyday of flannel-wearing grunge gods like Nirvana and Pearl Jam. Following one particularly dreadful Sunday worship set by a well-intended guy whose singing sounded like he was being electrocuted, Brad had had enough and asked to take over the worship. He soon showed up with a bunch of guys from his old band who smelled like cigarettes, including a guy with long hair and another guy with tattoos. So things looked very promising.

Adjusting to the new room at the fundamentalist church was tough. The acoustics were deplorable because the room was not designed for live rock. The echo was so bad that some people thought the electric guitar players were on reverb when they weren't. The hardest thing was controlling the drum kit volume because the drummer used what appeared to be baseball bats instead of drumsticks and beat the kit as if it were Rodney King. Somebody suggested that we could do what other churches did and put up a plastic shield in front of the drummer to control the volume, but the drummer threatened to quit and refused to be caged in like a zoo animal. So we just let them bring a hard rock flavor for our Savior. Man, the band was so good that our little church service really started to come together, and a lot of musicians started showing up because they appreciated the band.

The preaching, however, was still pretty brutal. We were trying to be a church without a primary leader and wanted to have Mike, Lief, and me co-pastor the church and share the pulpit. I preached topical sermons that were nothing more than doctrinal lectures filled with big theological words that nobody understood. Mike, an ex-jock, preached as if he were a football coach giving a motivational speech at halftime and said "you know" every third word. And no matter what the text was, Lief always had the same two points: (1) You suck. (2) You need to change.

Because the preaching had no continuity from week to week, people were confused. Lief was running a construction company, and Mike was running a campus ministry at the University of Washington, so I was the only person focusing full-time on the church. I really wanted to just take the pulpit and figure out how to preach by doing it every week, but I also wanted to respect these older, more seasoned, and very godly men. In time, they sat me down and said that they believed in me, wanted to cover my back, and wanted me to take the pulpit and lead the church.

This was one of the most important things that ever happened to me in ministry. I was young and filled with great hope and terrible fear. To some degree, I had been wrongly allowing Mike and Lief to shoulder the burden because I feared failure and hoped to share the blame if things went poorly. But I also knew that God had spoken to me and had clearly called me to lead the church. Their humility and support gave me enough faith to step up, take the pulpit, and lead the church. In retrospect, it is a testament to the character of these men that they supported me. They could have easily split our little church three ways but instead laid down their own power for the best interest of our mission to bring the gospel to Seattle. To this day, I thank God for both men.

When I started to preach nearly every week, I slowly got better as I figured out my own style and started to include my own peculiar sarcasm. In time, I became more comfortable and was able to preach without relying on my notes and began to use my humor to make my points, which allowed my personality to finally come through in the sermons. Admittedly, my preaching was not that good for a few years yet, but I was encouraged that at least I had progressed from really bad to just bad.

I began reading biographies of legendary preachers and learned that anointed preaching can only flow out of an anointed preacher who spends time alone with God in prayer and Scripture.[3] I also started studying stand-up comedians because, besides preachers, they are the only people in our culture who stand on a stage and speak to an audience for an extended period of time. In my opinion, Chris Rock is the most skilled comedic communicator alive today, and some years later, my wife bought us good seats to see him live, which was a better study in homiletics than most classes on the subject.

Anyway, our church started as a Bible study with a handful of people, and over the course of about six months, it grew to be a good weekly service of about seventy people, with a great band, child care, and hope.

Then the summer came. In Seattle the weather is darker than an Edgar Allen Poe story for about nine months of the year. But the summers are glorious. So people spend their summers outdoors, soaking up every minute of sun they can before the suicidal rains of fall overtake them.

Unfortunately, our little church met at 6:00 p.m. on Sunday nights in a hot church without air-conditioning, and the attendance started thinning to the degree that it looked like some of us had missed the rapture. I feared that if we did not do something creative, the church could easily shrink back down to a few dozen people.

Scrambling for ideas, I agreed to cancel a Sunday church service to let some of our long-haired public-radio types take us outside to do a large joint art project they had proposed. They gave each of us a large chunk of paper on which to paint something that symbolized our personality, which they would then string together as a large mural highlighting the different personalities in our church. As a truck-driving jock who watches a lot of Ultimate Fighting, I can honestly say it was the gayest thing I have ever been a part of. I feared ending up with a church of chickified arty dudes drinking herbal tea and standing around talking about their feelings, as illustrated by their finger painting. To this day, I twitch like a Vietnam vet just thinking about the mural.

So instead of murals, we started a midweek outdoor Bible study at a park across from the church we were meeting at. We met there each week for barbecue, volleyball, Frisbee golf, acoustic guitar worship, and a Bible study that I taught. Fortunately, this idea worked. People liked hanging out together, the handful of little kids we had wrestled with the college students, people brought their friends, and passersby often joined in with us. Through this simple weekly event, we not only held our people together but actually grew a little bit, and we learned that churches can grow in the summer.

As the summer was winding down, we were preparing for a big fall launch of our little church plant on the first Sunday in October 1996. I was feeling encouraged — until all hell broke loose and nearly killed us.

Reformission Reflections

1. Which type(s) of people likely feel most welcome in your church or ministry? Why?

2. Which type(s) of people likely feel least welcome in your church or ministry? What could be done to actively welcome those people?

3. Why do people come to your church or ministry? What draws them in and keeps them committed?

4. Why do people leave your church or ministry? Should anything be done to be more welcoming to those people who leave your church or ministry?

5. What agendas and missions that differ from that of your church or ministry have people tried to bring in? Were these ideas welcomed or rejected? What were the consequences of these people staying or leaving?

6. On a scale of 1 to 10, with 1 being poor and 10 being excellent, how good are the attractional elements of preaching and worship music at your church? What could be done to improve those scores?

7. On a scale of 1 to 10, with 1 being poor and 10 being excellent, how good is your church or ministry at equipping and sending people out to be missionaries where they live?

CHAPTER THREE

I was living with my boyfriend until I got saved. We got married and now I'm a deacon coordinating weddings.

Jesus, Satan Showed Up
and I Can't Find My Cup

75 – 150 People

A few weeks before we launched our little church plant in the fall of 1996, I was perplexed by an older man who had become something of a mentor to me. He was pushing some theological ideas that I did not agree with, such as ministers in skirts. But I was conflicted. On one hand, I really liked the idea of having a seasoned older pastor in the church to help compensate for my inexperience. On the other hand, my very discerning wife had the same Ghost check in her gut as I did. So since it was ultimately Jesus' church, we began praying that God would reveal to us what we should do about this man who wanted to be a pastor in the church and oversee our discipleship process.

The first clue that something was funky came when I let him preach his first sermon in our church. He brought his wife up to team teach with him, something I had not agreed to. As they were teaching, he told the story of Jesus' triumphal entry into Jerusalem on the back of an ass in fulfillment of Old Testament prophecy. He actually pulled me up onto the stage in front of the church and asked me to get on my hands and knees to play the part of the ass. The move seemed like an overt power play and was at least mildly disrespectful. I remembered Paul's command not to rebuke an older man harshly and quietly wondered if that included punching one in the mouth.

The second clue came in the form of a prophetic dream. I had never had a prophetic dream. I actually was not sure that such miraculous things still happened and was skeptical of prophetic dreams altogether. But while I was sleeping one night, the Holy Spirit gave me a dream in which I was standing in the foyer of our rented church on the opening night of our church plant. As I turned around in my dream, the older man walked in by himself, carrying a Bible in a brown leather case and wearing a blue shirt, green shorts, sandals, and a homemade cross around his neck. He informed me that he wanted to pastor the church and that I should step aside and let him. God then spoke Acts 20:28 – 31 to me, saying, "Keep watch over yourselves and all the flock of which the Holy Spirit has made you overseers. Be shepherds of the church of God, which he bought with his own blood. I know that after I leave, savage wolves will come in among you and will not spare the flock. Even from your own number men will arise and distort the truth in order to draw away disciples after them. So be on your guard!"

God then spoke through 1 Peter 5:1 – 4: "To the elders among you, I appeal as a fellow elder, a witness of Christ's sufferings and one who also will share in the glory to be revealed: Be shepherds of God's flock that is under your care, serving as overseers — not because you must, but because you are willing, as God wants you to be; not greedy for money, but eager to serve; not lording it over those entrusted to you, but being examples to the flock. And when the Chief Shepherd appears, you will receive the crown of glory that will never fade away."

I then woke up to tell my wife that God had revealed to me that the older man was a wolf sent by Satan and that Jesus wanted me to protect and lead the small flock he had given me. We prayed together. The next day I told Mike, Lief, and another pastor-buddy named Greg about the dream and asked them to hold it in confidence. Since that time, I have had many other similar dreams and words from God and always know they are from God because they come true and are confirmed by God with Scripture.

My wife, Grace, and I fasted and prayed for the week leading up to our first public church service. The only advertising we could afford was invitations we had printed up for our people to give to friends and family, but we were hoping for a big turnout.

On the opening night of our church plant in October of 1996, the service was just getting started when my wife realized that she had forgotten her Bible in the foyer. I jumped up to get it, and as I turned around, I found myself standing alone in the foyer, just as I had been in my dream. The older man then walked in the door wearing the same outfit he had worn in the dream and came toward me speaking every word he had in my dream. I was so stunned that I was momentarily speechless.

When I collected my thoughts, I told him to leave our church and never come back. A few months later, another older pastor contacted me and said that the man God warned me of had been kicked out of his denomination on suspicion of undermining young pastors and taking money from young churches.

After kicking the man out, I walked down the church aisle and handed my wife her Bible on my way up to preach from Acts 17 about Paul on Mars Hill—the name and ministry philosophy for our church. Between 160 and 200 people had shown up for our big kickoff service. The room was really dark, we had a lot of candles, and the music was very cool if you were into suicide. One of our long-haired arty types turned all the lights off and read Nietzsche's "The Madman" by candlelight, which was supposed to make us very bohemian and cool but just kind of scared the handful of normal people in attendance. The following week we leveled off at around 80 to 100 people as the friends, family, and well-wishers who came for the launch went back to their churches. Then the hard work began.

Our people did not know the Bible, and I kept trying to teach them systematic theology through the Sunday sermons, which did not work. They were very skeptical of systematic theology and did not trust anyone stringing verses together. But they were willing to learn the Bible. So I decided to try to teach them a book of the Bible by going through it verse by verse. For some insane reason, I chose Ecclesiastes and absolutely butchered the book because learning to preach biblical theology with Ecclesiastes is harder than medical students learning surgery by operating on themselves.

We continued to meet on Sunday nights until Christmas, when some of the arty types started complaining that there was a preaching monologue instead of an open dialogue, as would become popular with some emerging pastors a few years later. This forced me to think through my theology of preaching, spiritual authority, and the authority of Scripture. I did an intense study of the Old Testament prophets and the New Testament commands regarding preaching and teaching. In the end, I decided not to back off from a preaching monologue but instead to work hard at becoming a solid long-winded, old-school Bible preacher that focused on Jesus. My people needed to hear from God's Word and not from each other in collective ignorance like some dumb chat room.

After the prophetic dream from God, I thought we were in the clear and that Satan had been exposed so that we could continue growing our church. But enemy fire just kept coming.

All of our musicians except Brad started pushing a theological agenda that read pretty much like a lot of the nonsense being bantered about by some emerging pastors today, trying to reinvent Christian orthodoxy, which is by definition heresy. They decided that truth is relative, that all religions are right, that Jesus did not die as a substitute for our sin, and that everyone will likely go to heaven. They notified me of this during our church service when they stopped playing music to read texts from other religions.

In a tense confrontational meeting immediately after church, they droned on and on about how we needed to start having other religious leaders teach at our church in addition to me so that our church could embrace many religions and be true to our postmodern culture of pluralism. Because these musicians were not teachable, I kicked them out that night, and we went more than a month without any worship music in services. Some of the folks who had tried out as worship leaders during the core phase volunteered but were pretty horrible, so I decided to go without music until we sorted things out because silence is better than painful music.

One of our core values was beauty, and we had built much of our church identity on being cool and having good music, but suddenly we had nothing. So our church services were reduced to me preaching for about an hour, taking prayer requests, and closing in prayer. It was a brutal time. I decided that being cool, having good music, understanding postmodern epistemology, and welcoming all kinds of strange people into the church is essentially worthless if at the bedrock of the church anything other than a rigorous Jesus-centered biblical theology guides the mission of the church. And I needed to labor to continually improve as a Bible preacher because there is enough power in the preaching of God's Word alone to build a church from nothing. It seemed that we were in a spiritual war and that if light was going to spread throughout our dark city, it would have to emanate from the pulpit.

To make matters worse, one of our most talented leaders started embracing a postmodern hermeneutic and was trying to convince our people that the meaning of Scripture is relative and we should each have our own perspectives. Consequently, he also started taking carloads of our people, including newer converts, to a renegade mystical Catholic church in the mornings as well as to a New Age self-help cult during the week, which charged huge amounts of money to convince people that they were not sinners and could achieve anything they wanted through sheer will. He picked up this nonsense at a seminary where the Bible interpretation professor ended up being more postmodern than Christian. The professor wound up getting divorced a few times, which just proved to me that often people who mess with the Bible want to sin instead of repent, which explains why they bury Scripture under philosophical fads (Rom. 1:18).

In retrospect, this season was marked by intense spiritual warfare and demonic attacks that nearly killed me and the church. I had naively gathered people into our church but was not discerning as to who should be allowed to lead and influence others. Just as I thought we were coming together, things began to fall apart and heretics were seeking to hijack our gospel, false teachers were seeking to hijack our mission, and nutjobs were seeking to hijack our people. I painfully learned the importance of evaluating people, and over the years I have noticed various kinds of people who come into the church.

COACHING CORNER

People who come into a church need to be assessed so that the church leaders can identify who they are and what they need.

- **Horses** are vibrant leaders who pull a lot of weight and run fast. Horses need to have character, sound doctrine, and agree with the vision of the church.
- **Colts** are emerging leaders who need training, testing, and opportunities to lead. If properly broken in, a colt can be developed into a horse.
- **Fish** are non-Christians who are spiritually lost and often not actively looking for God. Fish need a Christian friend to lovingly introduce them to Jesus and his church.
- **Eagles** are skilled leaders who are being developed within the church with the express kingdom purpose of leaving the proverbial nest and leading a ministry elsewhere, such as missions work and church planting.
- **Mules** are faithful workers who dependably and continually do whatever is asked of them in the church. Mules need to be thanked and protected from burnout.
- **Cows** are selfish people who wander from church to church, chewing up resources without ever giving back to the church until they kill it. A fence needs to be built around the church to keep the cows out.
- **Squirrels** are people who are generally liked because they are nice, but they rarely do anything meaningful. Squirrels need to be put to work in the church.
- **Stray cats** are socially peculiar loners who linger around the church. Stray cats need a friend to help bring them into the church and an opportunity to serve other people so that they can be meaningfully connected to the church.

- **Rats** are people who appear to have the potential to have a fruitful ministry, but they lack dependability, humility, or maturity. Rats need to be rebuked, and if they do not repent, they must be strategically ignored until they commit to no longer being a waste of time and effort.
- **Sheep** are people who have legitimate needs that require patient and loving support. Examples of sheep include widows, orphans, and those who are seriously ill or fighting addictions. Sheep need to be loved and served.
- **Ducks** are disgruntled people who continually quack about whatever they are unhappy about. Ducks need to stop quacking, or the pastor(s) must go duck hunting before the ducks drown out everyone and everything else in the church.
- **Wolves** are false teachers whom Satan sends into the church to devour Jesus' sheep. Wolves need to be quickly identified, rebuked, and if they are unrepentant, they must be shot before their false teaching destroys people in the church.
- **Snakes** are evil people sent by the Serpent on a mission to destroy the church through anything from sexual sin to starting rumors. Leaders must stomp on the heads of snakes before they bite people and infect them with deadly venom.

During this season, I was unsure that our church would survive. The artists who had left really hurt our reputation in their circles of influence. The variety of heretics we had in our church caused some local churches to wonder if we weren't a cult with candles, depressing music, and an inexperienced young pastor who said "dude" a lot. And the soft church people from our core group started to wilt under the pressure.

I hit a particularly low point one day when a young couple knocked on the door of our home. We had invested hundreds of hours in the young woman, dating back to our college ministry. Her husband was a new Christian whom she had met in the church.

We had done their premarital counseling, and I had officiated their wedding. When they got married, they could not even afford a couch, so I drove one of ours over in my truck and gave it to them. We considered them friends until they came over to tell us they had left the church. They complained that since the church had grown a bit bigger and things a bit busier, my wife and I had become less available to them.

My wife and I were both working other jobs because the church could not pay me and were volunteering more than forty hours a week to the church. Being rejected by friends felt like a punch in the gut.

We were stunned. We needed couples like this to help the church survive, not jump ship just because my wife could not drop everything to take this woman out to tea whenever was convenient for her. The odd thing was that they transferred to a megachurch in the suburbs, which made no sense because they would get no closer to that pastor and his wife than they had to Grace and me. Yet they knocked on our door unannounced to tell us we were not doing enough for them. It seemed obvious to me that they wanted us to bend over backward and promise to do anything to make them happy in order to keep them in the church. But I simply gave up and sent them on their way because they were not on our mission to bring the gospel to Seattle. For them, the mission was to get Grace and me to jump like trained dogs upon command.

In retrospect, this was a hard lesson, one that I have had to learn many times in the various seasons of our church. As a church grows, it also changes. And as a church changes, so does the accessibility of the pastor and his family. As the pastor gets busier with new people and responsibilities, some people are displaced and are not as close to the pastor as they had been. Displaced people are prone to expect the pastor to ensure that their access to him and his family will never change. If the pastor agrees to these demands, he will keep the disgruntled people but not reach any new people because the mission will shift from reaching new people to pleasing old people.

No matter what leaders in this situation do, they will lose people and must wisely choose who they will lose.

By this time, we had morphed into two different congregations. Half of the people were committed to building a church that brought the gospel to the city and were willing to faithfully serve that mission. The other half of the people were mainly young, burned-out church kids who wanted to be cool, have an artists enclave, and deconstruct everything remotely Christian.

As an ex-baseball player, I realized that with all the craziness in the church, I needed to be the umpire. Some years later at a Leadership Network event, I had dinner with the church growth Yoda, Lyle Schaller. He told a story about an old umpire he had met. He asked the umpire how he felt after making the wrong call. The umpire stated that he never made a wrong call. Puzzled, Schaller asked if he truly believed that he had never called a safe man out, an out man safe, a ball a strike, or a strike a ball. The umpire said that he had never made a bad call. Schaller asked him how that could be, and the umpire simply said, "It ain't nothing until I call it."

In my church, I had heretics calling themselves Christians, and I had lazy, selfish Christians calling themselves mature. I needed to start making the calls. So I started meeting with people one-on-one and calling them everything from sinners who needed to repent, to leaders who needed to lead, to heretics who needed to leave. It was a brutal season, but I kept going back to my dream in which God said the problems would come from within the church and I was supposed to lead the church and obey Jesus, who was our Senior Pastor.

Though our church was brand-new, we had already lost focus of our mission, and people were debating if the heretics should have been kicked out and other things that were a waste of time. So I decided to create a crisis that would force everyone to focus on a mission and pull together to accomplish a task. I have learned that sometimes the most important thing a leader can do is to create strategic chaos that forces people to pull together and focus on an urgent need, thereby subtly getting rid of all their other missions and complaints in a subversive way.

Our attendance had declined to about sixty or seventy people, and those who remained liked our little church meeting by candlelight in a lovely old church on Sunday nights and would have been happy to continue forever without much change. So I moved our church out of our nice little building right before Christmas with only a few weeks notice in an effort to shake things up and give us a fresh start in a new place some twenty minutes away. The neighborhood we moved to is a few miles from the University of Washington and is a ritzy type of place where all the kids, named Buffy and Biff, spend their days learning Latin while being driven around by their nanny. A Presbyterian church there had died, and we rented their vacant church building. We finally got a few offices but had to keep our service at 6:00 p.m. because an Asian church met there in the morning.

In the move, we lost some of our least-committed people, as I was hoping we would. We were able to set up part of the building as if it were our own. We actually got to put a sign out front, which was a big deal because it felt like we were stabilizing. We also got to paint the classrooms, set up our nursery rooms, leave our sound system set up, hang paintings on the walls, and use the beautiful classic church sanctuary with wooden pews and wooden arches as a lovely space for a dark, arty evening service by candlelight.

In the new building, we finally opened an office and hired a part-time secretary, which was a huge relief. But I failed to compile a formal job description, conduct a formal interview process, or conduct regular evaluations, which caused frustration for both me and the young woman I hired. The truth is that while I knew I needed some support staff in the office to make the bank deposits, answer the phone, take in the mail, return the email, and so on, I did not really know how to hire or manage a staff.

We also began having dinner together as a church on Wednesday nights, with a handful of classes and Bible studies scattering throughout the building after the meal. Mike started a film and theology discussion group. Previously we had a few Bible studies meeting in homes throughout the city that were doing okay because they were taught by Mike, Lief, and me. But we really had no place to relationally connect new people until Wednesday night opened up. It cemented relationships in our church and quickly connected some new people into friendships. It also allowed theological training for our newer Christians, which would help protect us from further attacks by false teachers.

We still lacked a worship leader. But on some weeks a guy named Dave Bazan played guitar and sang when he was not touring with his band, Pedro the Lion.

Within a few months, Brad pulled together enough new musicians for another band, and all we lacked was a drummer. So I decided to empty the church bank account and buy a brand-new custom-built drum kit. Week after week, we set up the kit in the center of the stage for the church service and did not allow anyone to play it. Because of my insecurity, I had until now worked very hard to conceal our needs in an effort to give the impression that we had everything together. But I decided our needs would never be filled unless we made them visible. So I placed the shiny green, virgin drum kit up as the centerpiece of our worship set each week and prayed that a drummer would eventually ask me why no one was playing it.

Then Matt introduced himself. He had attended a few times to check us out. Matt was a tall, slender, hip-looking, punk-rock guy with greased-back hair, kind of like a neo–*Happy Days* dude. He has played on more albums for Tooth and Nail Records than any other musician in the history of the label, for punk bands such as Plankeye and Roadside Monument. He asked why we did not have a drummer playing the drum kit, and I explained that I was praying for a guy like him to volunteer. He offered to play and is flat out one of the most amazing drummers I have ever heard.

Additionally, he turned out to be a godly man who to this day remains a dear friend, a Bible study leader, and a drummer in our church. Once Matt joined us, we suddenly gained credibility again with a lot of folks in the music scene, and before long, other good musicians were checking us out since Matt was our missionary into their tribe. Finally we had a band again, were in a new building that was pretty cool, had some offices, had a midweek event going, and were getting some traction.

At the time, I was wrestling through some theological issues, such as election, predestination, and other matters generally known as reformed theology. So I taught through the book of Romans on Sunday nights, which helped to clarify our doctrinal convictions as a church and cemented us as a church with a reformed view of God and salvation. If you don't know what that means, the gist is that people suck and God saves us from ourselves. For more details, you can read the book I'll write on it in the future or just accept a plain, literal reading of Romans, particularly Romans 9–11.

Anyway, we began to grow again and went from 80 people to around 130 in about nine months. It really felt as if we had turned a corner. One Sunday night we had our biggest attendance since our launch and ballooned to perhaps 150 in our room that could hold only a few more people than that. It was the first time people needed to sit in the balcony because the main floor was full, and the room was buzzing with excitement.

At the beginning of one church service, one of our leaders was up front leading the church in a time of prayer. Various people prayed aloud for our city and church. I was sitting with my wife, Grace, when God spoke to me and told me to go to the front of the church. So I got up and walked to the front of the church. Since everyone's heads were bowed and eyes were closed in prayer, no one seemed to notice my getting up. I felt awkward but stood there for a few moments, when a young man whom I had not seen before started praying from the back of the room.

Suddenly his voice changed and got very loud and authoritative, commanding us to stop worshiping Jesus and trust in ourselves instead. He stood up and looked me in the eye with a crazy look and sprinted down the center aisle of the church, spouting absolute heresy about Jesus. I stood in the center aisle and quickly opened my Bible to 1 John 4:1–6 and read aloud the section on false spirits sent into the world by Satan to spew falsehood about Jesus. The crazed man stopped in his tracks inches before me, breathing heavily.

I raised my hand to pray against the demon in the man and to ask Jesus to save him. The man turned and sprinted down the center aisle, throwing open two sets of doors on his way out as he ran into the street screaming.

At first, a number of people in the church thought this was yet another weird arty skit or object lesson dreamed up by our long-haired public-radio types. But once people looked up to see my face, it was obvious that this was not a planned event, which caused many people to be rightfully fearful.

Admittedly, I was a bit freaked out myself. I had been raised Roman Catholic, met Jesus in college, where I attended a tame Evangelical Free Church, and then moved to Seattle, where I worked with college students at an independent Bible church. My church experience had generally taught me that the supernatural craziness in Acts had ceased and was no longer operating. So I had never seen anything like this, and no one had ever given me pointers about the protocol for dealing with a demonized dude in a church service.

My answer to everything is pretty much the same: open the Bible and preach about the person of Jesus and his mission for our church. So I skipped my planned sermon from Romans that night and used the moment to explain the mission of our church.

I told the church that we could view the demon-possessed man either as our enemy or as our mission. I explained that God had allowed him to enter our church and exposed his condition in an effort to break our hearts because our Enemy had enslaved many people like that young man. Therefore, we needed to be a church intensely committed to Scripture because it alone was the weapon that could defeat our Enemy and liberate people. I explained that we needed to have our hearts broken so that we would weep for the condition of our city as Jesus wept over Jerusalem. I taught that if Satan was willing to attack our little church service, it confirmed that God had us in Seattle for an enormous mission and that the Enemy was trying to destroy us while we were small, just like Herod tried to kill Jesus when he was only an infant. I ended by explaining that in Romans 8:28, God promises to work all things for our good if we love him, and Genesis 50:20 says that what was meant for evil will be used by God for good and for the saving of many lives.

I called our people to join in our mission to follow Jesus into war for the heart of our city and closed in prayer. I wept in front of my church for the first time as the magnitude of what we were doing hit me at a level deeper than ever before. I had never opened my eyes while I prayed before our church, and for the first time, I prayed with my eyes open because I felt God had opened our eyes that night. My people had their heads bowed in silence, and it absolutely broke me to know that these people were entrusted to my leadership and care. I hoped that we had witnessed the first shot of a war that would end with Jesus standing on the neck of our Enemy in the middle of our city for everyone to see.

The demonized guy later returned to the church, and Mike and Lief followed up with him and his unsaved friend. The demonized young man did not recall what had happened, and his friend said he had never seen his buddy act like that before and was worried for him. Mike and Lief shared the gospel with the young men, who were very spiritually confused, and prayed for them before they left, never to return again.

The following week, our attendance dropped a bit since the large number of visitors had been understandably weirded out by the demonic dude. But those who stayed with us had a new resolve that the heretics, false teachers, and other problems we had recently fought through were all Satan's way of sidetracking us from the simplicity of the gospel but that Jesus had spared us for a great work in our city. Some people started gathering informally on Sundays to pray for our church and city. A number of people stopped playing church and started owning our mission to reach our city and see Jesus transform our culture. The demonic event caused another buzz to go out about our church, and more people started dropping in to see what was going on, so we grew back up to around 150 people within a few months.

During the summer, we continued our midweek outdoor Bible study but moved it to a new park just off a waterway that was heavily trafficked by boaters. People sat on a grassy area under a large totem pole, while the band and I stood on a dock. It was a beautiful setting with boats passing by and the sun setting over Lake Washington. We baptized new converts in the water while everyone cheered.

The only problem ended up being the boaters. I could not see what was going on behind me because my back was to the water while I was teaching. During our first meeting, our people kept waving at boaters who passed by, which was annoying but kind of cute. One evening a few weeks into the study, no one was looking at me while I taught, and everyone had troubled looks on their faces. I turned around to see a bunch of frat guys with their shorts around their ankles, mooning my church as what was apparently one of their dad's boats passed by. It was tough to preach with a backdrop of hairy heinies.

A few weeks later, I again noticed that no one was looking at me while I preached and turned around to see a few well-endowed young women passing by on a boat, lifting up their shirts like Mardi Gras princesses as they flashed our Bible study. I used the moment to say something about choosing the location because of its natural beauty but not anticipating that much natural beauty and went on to say something about total depravity and how only in our city could we be flashed at a Bible study.

Not surprisingly, the Bible study did grow for two main reasons. First, our people and their friends liked the fact that they could smoke during the Bible study since it was outdoors. Some people got saved at the study, including three people who later became deacons and one person who became an elder, all because they could smoke at church. Two of the people who got saved were a stripper and her live-in boyfriend, whom I later married on the same dock. Second, the word got out that there were naked women at our Bible study, which seemed to be a plus when inviting lost friends.

I tried to finish up the Bible study with dignity, planning to move it to another park the following summer to avoid the naked hecklers. I thought we had made it through the summer without any more trauma—until the last week of the summer study. As I was finishing my message, a boat went by with what looked to be about half of the church onboard, drinking heavily and yelling loudly. The boat was driven by the same guy who kept taking our people to the renegade mystical Catholic Church and the New Age self-help cult seminars, and he had my secretary with him, which was, to say the least, troubling. It proved to be the beginning of a season of dealing with widespread immaturity.

Reformission Reflections

1. What are some of the most bizarre things you have seen in a church or ministry?

2. How has Satan tried to destroy your church or ministry? How successful was his plan?

3. Which types of people in the Coaching Corner list are currently getting the most attention in your church or ministry?

4. Which type of people in the Coaching Corner list do you most appreciate? Why? Which do you least appreciate? Why?

5. Without naming names, describe people that come to mind as illustrations of the various kinds of people listed in the Coaching Corner.

6. How would you categorize yourself based on the Coaching Corner list? Are you proud of that, or do you need to make some life changes?

7. Based on the Coaching Corner list, which kind of person do you most aspire to be? Why?

CHAPTER FOUR

I was a pothead until I got saved and now I am the president of the chamber of commerce and the executive pastor.

Jesus, Could You Please Rapture the Charismaniac Lady Who Brings Her Tambourine to Church?

150–350 People

I swore the young mother was going to pull out a wooden spoon, put me over her knee, and whoop me right in the middle of our church service. She apparently lived near the church, and our worship band blaring through our honking speakers woke up her kid who was napping. At the time, we did not have ushers or greeters to keep things in order, so the irate mother pushed the stroller right into our sanctuary, she and her kid both screaming at the top of their lungs in hellish harmony.

Apparently, we had quickly worn out our welcome in the new church building nestled among the homes of millionaires. We had no parking, so our assortment of beater cars and mopeds clogged all of the previously quiet streets in the neighborhood. Our neighbors particularly appreciated it when, for example, an old Datsun worth less than the tank of gas in an SUV blocked said SUV in its driveway.

To make matters worse, some lug nut spray painted "Mars Hill Rules" on the pristine white church, on the side of the building that faces the main street, of course. Before long, the police were regularly being called to tow cars and to cite us for noise violations. Each time, the cop would show up, wipe the donut glaze off his face, smile, and check the volume level of our worship service with a noise meter. Not once did he ever find that we had exceeded the legal noise limit, which is basically equivalent to Metallica playing live in an elevator. We eventually got our own noise meter to regulate our volume, and we put up signs around the neighborhood asking our people not to park illegally, which they respected.

By the end of the summer of 1997, we were running anywhere between 120 and 150 people on Sundays, and the sanctuary was looking fairly full. We were doing pretty well except for the one dreadful night we tried out hip-hop worship on a bunch of white indie rocker kids. Worse still, it was the only night that the very elderly former secretary of the Presbyterian church that owned the building dropped in to visit, and she left shaking her head without making eye contact with me. She kept an office on-site and had final control over our use of the building. From that point forward, we got along as pleasantly as a bitterly divorced couple still living under the same roof.

We survived the horrendous holy hip-hop havoc and expanded to two Sunday services in time for the fall push, which is when historically we have seen our biggest attendance increase. Since we still could not find a Sunday morning location, we decided to split our 6:00 p.m. service into two services, one at 5:00 p.m. and one at 7:00 p.m.

In his "Rule of 150," Malcolm Gladwell states that the highest number of people the average person can connect with is 150.[1] This helps explain why many groups cease growing at that number. For example, the Methodist movement of John Wesley collected people into communities of about 150.[2] In twenty-one hunter-gatherer societies, the average village had 148.4 people.[3] Most military fighting units are under 200, and Hutterite communities grow no larger than 150 by design.[4] Therefore, any congregation committed to evangelism and the expansion of its ministry should expect to find it difficult to grow beyond this number.

When I told our people that we were going to grow beyond 150 people and expand to two services, some of them freaked out. The most common complaint was that we would no longer have real community because people attending different services would never meet. What they were really saying is that they wanted to be a small community and not a large community of multiple smaller communities.

I explained to them that in Acts 1 the early church was about our size and was meeting together with great unity and gladness. Then in Acts 2, the Holy Spirit dropped on Pentecost, 3,000 people were saved, and they never again met as a little church of 120 people in the upper room. I explained that if the early church had the same attitude that our church had, the gospel would not have spread and we would have never heard about Jesus. I made it clear that limiting the size of the church for our convenience was a sin and that we should be a church that always exists more for the people who are not yet saved than for the people who are.

Because our people had grown to increasingly trust the Scriptures and our mission, they went along with the change to two services. In doing so, they were repenting of their selfishness, and God honored their repentance. In retrospect, I believe this was one of the most important moments in the history of our church because we were deciding if Mars Hill Church was to be defined by the size of its mission to reach the lost or by the number of people we could gather at one time in one room.

I can still remember how nervous I was on the first week of our big transition. Would people all go to one service and leave the other empty? Would we lose people by eliminating the 6:00 p.m. service they were accustomed to? Thankfully, the attendance split evenly between the two services, and we jumped up to about 160 people immediately. Through this, I learned that when you give people more options, more of them opt, and growth happens.

At that time, I preached what I think was my first decent sermon series because it was very practical and I had finally started to learn how to connect every passage of Scripture to Jesus. Our church was still nearly all college students and singles, with a few young married couples and families with small children mixed in. I assumed the students and singles were all pretty horny, so I went out on a limb and preached through the Song of Songs in the fall. I printed up a nice lengthy introduction to the book, with a lot of information about sex and marriage. Each week I handed out sermon notes with commentary on the book.

The Bible simply tells us to "preach the Word" (2 Tim. 4:2) and does not tell us exactly how this should be done. Occasionally we do see Jesus preaching very long sermons (Matt. 15:29 – 32), as well as Paul (Acts 20:7 – 11). But we do not have transcripts of their sermons to see exactly what was said.

We know from church history that such influential preachers as Justin Martyr preached expository sermons that went through books of the Bible line by line. At Mars Hill, we occasionally preach topics that need to be addressed, but the majority of the preaching simply goes through books of the Bible chapter by chapter and verse by verse, rotating between Old and New Testament books as God leads. The key, however, is to move through the Bible books fairly quickly rather than lingering forever in a book by drilling down on every word to the degree that the people in the church lose sight of the overarching mega-themes and purposes of the book.

I believe preaching through books of the Bible is beneficial for a number of reasons. First, it is important for Christians to learn all of Scripture and not just topics. Second, it is important for Christians to learn how to study a book of the Bible and how God inspired it to be organized and interconnected. Third, with so many new believers and non-Christians visiting Mars Hill, it is important that we teach in a way that allows them to follow along without getting lost as they try to jump around in their Bibles. Fourth, because all Scripture is God-breathed and for our benefit, there is not a page of Scripture that is not helpful to our faith, so we should examine it all. Fifth, going through books of the Bible forces us to examine tough and controversial issues that we may otherwise ignore. Sixth, because our people easily connect with narrative teaching styles, a biblical and narrative teaching of the Bible most easily connects with their learning style as long as the Bible is presented as one unified story with Jesus as the hero.

Each sermon on the Song of Songs took more than an hour and began a trend of long sermons that sometimes creep to an hour and a half or more. Each week I extolled the virtues of marriage, foreplay, oral sex, sacred stripping, and sex outdoors, just as the book teaches, because all Scripture is indeed profitable. I was frank but not crass and did not back away from any of the tough issues regarding sex and pleasure. This helped us a lot because apparently a pastor using words like "penis" and "oral sex" is unusual, and before you could say "aluminum pole in the bedroom," attendance began to climb steadily to more than two hundred people a week. Additionally, a lot of people got engaged, and young wives started showing up with big baby bellies, a trend that has continued unabated ever since. After much work and many mistakes, we had finally grown to the adolescent phase of church.[5]

A buzz got out about our church, and Christian pastors and leaders from around the country and the world began dropping in to check out what we were doing. One such person was a young unknown author named Donald Miller, who came to visit us from Portland. He seemed to like what we were doing and asked if we had any churches in Portland. He was a really nice guy struggling to make ends meet running a small publishing company out of his apartment.

Eventually a young pastor named Rick McKinley, who has become a very dear friend, planted a church in Portland for our

COACHING CORNER

Adolescence is achieved after the long and painful season of doing the hard work it takes to get a church functioning with healthy systems, competent leaders, and clear expectations of people. This season is marked by a number of critical beginnings, such as getting the wrong people out of the church and getting the right people to commit to the church and to doing whatever it takes to accomplish the mission. Getting to this phase is exhausting, and if the leaders' plans fail, they lose credibility and the church settles into a lethargic state of decline.

Acts 29 Network, and Donald helped him get it started. The church is doing great, and so is Donald. His book *Blue Like Jazz* has taken off as the cult classic for young emerging Christians.[6] When it first came out, I was told that he had written about my involvement in his life, and I was filled with great pride to know that I had been noted in such a popular book. I grabbed a copy and thumbed through it to find that I'm only mentioned in a few sentences as Mark the cussing pastor. Yet again I felt like Charlie Brown trying to get his foot on the ball to no avail, but I still love Don nonetheless and won't cuss him out.

Around the time that other pastors began visiting us, I was invited to speak at my first pastors' conference, hosted by Leadership Network, at the Mount Hermon Conference Center in northern California. The topic was the then trendy and now embarrassing Generation X ministry. The speakers at the conference included Dieter Zander, who was at Willow Creek at the time trying to do something cool for young people, and Chris Seay, who was leading University Baptist Church in Texas. Chris has gone on to write a number of books and has become something of an icon in the emerging church.[7]

The worship leader for the conference was a skinny, hillbilly-looking young man whom Chris had been training, named David Crowder, who has gone on to write some worship songs that are very popular among emerging churches.[8] Dan Kimball, who later wrote *The Emerging Church* as well as other books, picked me up at the airport, sporting his cool rockabilly hairdo, and drove me to the conference.[9]

I had never been to a pastors' conference and was a bit worried about what I was supposed to do. When I got there, I was relieved to see that it was attended mainly by clueless young high-fiving white guys with facial hair, like me.

In college I had studied philosophy under a Christian professor who did his thesis on Descartes and modern understandings of truth and knowledge. He got me reading philosophy, which led to a lengthy multiyear study of the transition from the modern to the postmodern world.[10] Because I was familiar with the growing curiosity about postmodernism, I spoke on these subjects. I titled my session "The Flight from God," which I stole from existential philosopher Max Picard's book by the same name.[11]

That message reportedly outsold any conference tape at Mount Hermon that year. And it shifted the conversation from reaching Generation X to the emerging mission of reaching postmodern culture. I was not prepared for the media onslaught that came shortly thereafter. Before I knew it, National Public Radio was interviewing me, *Mother Jones* magazine did a feature on our church, Pat Robertson's 700 Club gave me a plaque for being America's "Church of the Week" and did a television story on us, other media outlets started asking for interviews, large denominations were asking me to be a consultant despite the fact that I wasn't exactly sure what a consultant was, and conferences were calling and asking me to speak as an expert on things I did not know.

The church still was not paying me, so I was living off of outside support from another church. I was not making enough money to pull my wife out of work and start our family. So I started traveling a lot to speak at various conferences, hoping to help serve other Christian leaders and supplement my income.

Pretty soon Leadership Network hired a young pastor named Doug Pagitt, who later went on to help found the Emergent Network, to organize what they were calling the Young Leaders Network.[12] Our small team of young pastors started getting more media attention, more speaking opportunities, and even book offers from major Christian publishers. Before long, another pastor was added to our Young Leaders team who was a few years younger than my dad, which did not seem like a young leader. But he was genuinely nice. His name was Brian McLaren, and he has gone on to become a very successful writer with some very stimulating views and opinions.[13] And though I sincerely love Brian and appreciate the kindness he has shown me, I generally disagree with many of his theological conclusions. Because he comes from a pacifistic Brethren background, such things as power and violence greatly trouble him. His pacifism seems to underlie many of our theological disagreements since he has a hard time accepting such things as the violence of penal substitutionary atonement, parts of the Old Testament where God killed people, and the concept of conscious eternal torment in hell. Curiously, it is also Brian's pacifism that makes him such a warmly engaging person who is able to speak and write about theologically controversial issues while being gracious. Ironically, my love for and disagreement with Brian are both borne out of his pacifism. But I find it curious that, from my perspective, he is using his power as a writer and speaker to do violence to Scripture in the name of pacifism.

I was not accustomed to the traveling or to the evangelical subculture that I was thrust into. I would travel during the week to speak or consult and then hurry home in time to preach at our two growing church services. I quickly got burned-out, angry, and frustrated. Additionally, I was spiritually immature and would vent my anger from the stage, cussing people out and acting like a jerk on more than one occasion. Then the team of young pastors started raising questions about the sovereignty of God, God's knowledge of the future, calling God "she" instead of "he," whether Jesus died as a substitute for our sin, and some other crazy stuff that just made me angry. I felt that I was wasting my time arguing with young pastors over stuff that was clear to me in the Bible, I was not helping anyone by having a foul mouth and bad attitude, I was neglecting my wife, and I was not doing a good job of building my church into more than a cool event.

Within a few years, the Young Leaders Network disbanded and emerged briefly as the Terra Nova Project, led by Brian McLaren, Doug Pagitt, Tony Jones, and Andrew Jones. On the front page of their first Terra Nova website, they thanked Chris Seay and me for founding the movement, which made me uneasy because I did not want to be associated with the theological direction the movement was taking, though they were personally nice guys. Though it was hard to part company with these men, I believe that conviction must override community, and we were not theologically like-minded. The Terra Nova Project disbanded before long, and the Emergent Village replaced it.[14]

Back at my church, as the two evening services started to fill up, our attendance began bouncing somewhere in the 220 to 250 range on Sundays. I thought we were ready to launch an off-site service near the University of Washington. We had wanted to be close to the campus since the beginning of the church but had not been able to find a place to meet in that area. But now an opportunity opened up to start a 9:00 p.m. Sunday service next to the campus at a Vineyard church. Lief did not think it was a good idea, but I was convinced that we were on a roll and that I could pull it off.

So I grabbed one of our punk-rock worship teams that had recently come together, with Matt drumming, Jeff, who had been the front man for a punk band called 90 Pound Wuss, and a college student named Luke singing and playing guitar. They have remained with our church ever since as the worship team humorously called Team Strikeforce. I also grabbed a few young college students who wanted to go into ministry, expecting I could use the experience to train them.

But the new church service absolutely flopped, for many reasons. First, the event was alright, but I did not put together a core of missionaries and arrogantly thought people would just show up to the event because it was cool. Second, the punk worship band was incredible but did not fit the acoustic-guitar-Dave-Matthews-loving, Gap-wearing, frat-guy college scene. Third, drunk homeless guys kept wandering in and yelling at me about everything from UFOs to wheat bread while I tried to preach. Fourth, a few of the more peculiar people from the Vineyard church started showing up. Among them was an older woman who always wore purple because it is the biblical color of royalty, brought a praise flag, and carried a tambourine with ribbons flowing from it to jump on stage and play with the punk band as the Spirit led. One night I put my face in my hands during worship, asking Jesus to rapture her immediately. Fifth, 9:00 p.m. was obviously too late for a church service unless we were hosting a Vampires for Christ meeting.

I had failed to think missionally about who we would reach out with, who we would reach out to, or how we would reach out. Instead, I had wrongly thought only attractionally, believing that if I had a good band and I preached a good sermon, we could put together a good event that would attract lots of people all by itself. So I failed miserably. As this train wreck of a church service rolled along for a few months, it became painfully clear that I had no choice but to pull the plug and pronounce the death sentence.

To tell the truth, this was a shot to my dignity because I thought I could make it work and am not a guy who has failed very often in his life. In hindsight, I think God let the failure sting because he wanted me to learn to always do both missional and attractional ministry and not repeat this mistake again.

During this season, my wife, Grace, also started to experience a lot of serious medical problems. Her job was very stressful, and between her long hours at the office and long hours at the church, her body started breaking down. I felt tremendously convicted that I had sinned against my wife and had violated the spirit of 1 Timothy 5:8, which says that if a man does not provide for his family, he has denied his faith and has acted in a manner worse than that of an unbeliever. I repented to Grace for my sin of not making enough money and having her shoulder any of the financial burden for our family. We did not yet have elders installed in the church but did have an advisory council in place, and I asked them for a small monthly stipend to help us make ends meet, and I supplemented our income with outside support and an occasional speaking engagement.

Shortly thereafter, Grace gave birth to our first child, my sweetie pie Ashley. Up to this point, Grace had continuously poured endless hours into the church. She taught a women's Bible study, mentored many young women, oversaw hospitality on Sundays, coordinated meals for new moms recovering from birth, and organized all of the bridal and baby showers. Grace's dad had planted a church before she was born and has remained there for more than forty years. Her heart for ministry and willingness to serve was amazing. But as our church grew, I felt I was losing my wife because we were both putting so many hours into the church that we were not connecting as a couple like we should have. I found myself getting bitter against her because she would spend her time caring for our child and caring for our church but was somewhat negligent of me.

I explained to Grace that her primary ministry was to me, our child, and the management of our home and that I needed her to pull back from the church work to focus on what mattered most. She resisted a bit at first, shed a few tears, but in time realized that I took care of the church but no one took care of me but her. And the best thing she could do for the church was to make sure that we had a good marriage and godly children as an example for other people in the church to follow. It was the first time that I remember actually admitting my need for help to anyone. It was tough. But I feared that if we did not put our marriage and children above the demands of the church, we would end up with the lukewarm, distant marriage that so many pastors have because they treat their churches as mistresses that they are more passionate about than their brides.

As I began putting my home in order, I was also convicted that I had not yet put the church in order. Because we were meeting in the evenings, we started to see an increase in double-dipping churchgoers. They would attend their church in the morning and then drop in on our evening service because it was different and at least mildly cool. So we were growing in numbers but not in leaders or givers. The church was increasingly becoming simply an event that only a handful of people served at or gave to.

Although I was frustrated with both my wife and church, I had to own the fact that they both were under my leadership and that I had obviously done a poor job of organizing things to function efficiently. And since we did not yet have elders formally in place, there was no one to stop me from implementing dumb ideas like the 9:00 p.m. church service. So I decided to come to firmer convictions on church government and structure so that I could establish the founding framework for what our church leadership would look like. I spent hundreds of hours studying Scripture and church history and meeting with pastors from multiple theological traditions to hear their case and test it with Scripture. Some day I hope to write a thorough biblical and practical book on church leadership, but for the purposes of this book, I will briefly explain and practically critique the three most popular ecclesiological options and leave the theological heavy lifting for another time.

First I studied congregational ecclesiology, which is illustrated below.

Congregational Ecclesiology

In congregational ecclesiology, the congregation holds the highest authority in the church. Practically, this means that the congregation votes on church matters and that some form of majority rules, basically like a democracy. The entire concept seems to be taken from a secular volunteer organization that is run by volunteers but hires a small staff and a full-time director to run the day-to-day operations.

The staff and pastor are essentially seen as employees of the congregation, to be fired if they do not meet the expectations of their employer, the congregation. As I studied the Bible, I found more warrant for a church led by unicorns than by majority vote. Practically, it seemed obvious that a congregationally governed church would not be led but would instead make decisions by compromise to appease all of the various interests in the church. Moreover, it has been proven statistically that while congregationally governed churches tend to have longevity, they cannot grow very large because they lack a clear leader. And the thought of all of our young, newly saved, chain-smoking, unemployed porn addicts outvoting me on Jesus' will for our church sounded like the lunatics taking over the asylum. So I dismissed the congregational government option rather quickly.

I then explored the senior pastor ecclesiology option. In this model, the senior pastor is God's specially anointed man and functions as the highest authority in the church. Under the senior pastor is a staff that works for the pastor and is supposed to implement his vision for his church. The people in the congregation are the customers to be taken care of by the pastor and his staff.

Senior Pastor Ecclesiology

Pastor

Staff

Congregation

The senior pastor model borrows its organizational structure from corporate business, with a CEO, employees, and customers. Churches using this model have the potential to grow large quickly because they have simple and decisive leadership with only one senior leader. But they are also prone to make big mistakes since no one is able to stop a dumb idea or heretical doctrine if it comes from the senior pastor. And since the senior pastor is functionally not submissive or accountable to anyone, the church is very vulnerable to sin by the senior pastor, particularly sexual sin. In addition to not seeing this model as biblical, I also thought that, on a practical level, I would be putting my family and my church in danger if I was the solo senior leader because, to destroy the church, Satan would only need for me to commit an egregious sin or get hit by a car. So I rejected the senior pastor ecclesiology as both unbiblical and unwise.

I then began to study elder ecclesiology, which is what I had basically believed to be right since I first read the Bible as a new Christian. I found many things that I appreciated about the elder-governed model, including the principle of a team of senior leaders that were mutually submissive. Theologically, this made sense to me because it seemed more Trinitarian with a leadership community and took into account that pastors are capable of making simple mistakes and big sins just like everyone else and therefore need the insights and accountability of other qualified elders.

Elder Ecclesiology

I was disappointed, however, when I inspected elder-governed churches because they did not operate as a team of equals with a first-among-equals leader like I saw in the New Testament. Instead, a strong senior pastor still sat as the highest seat of authority in the church. The elders did function as peers of the senior pastor at the churches I investigated. But they were mainly unpaid volunteers who were good businessmen. They were generally godly but were not skilled pastors. They tended to function well in this system because it was much like the corporate business structure they were accustomed to, with a CEO, a board of directors, employees, and customers. But rather than functioning as fellow pastors with the senior pastor, they instead functioned more like a corporate board that approved the plans brought to them by the senior pastor and gave generously to help underwrite fundraising.

Under the elder board that focused on business were staff members who were recognized as pastors but not as elders. This did not make sense because the Bible uses the words interchangeably (e.g.,

Acts 20:28–29; 1 Peter 5:1–2). The staff pastors generally knew the Bible, the people in the church, and the day-to-day needs of the church far better than the men on the elder board who were leading them and making decisions they were supposed to implement. This often leads to great frustration between staff members and elder boards that are out of touch with what is really happening in the church.

As I considered these three options from a missional perspective, it seemed obvious to me that these models all shared numerous flaws. Among them are the following problems:

Jesus did not make the church organizational chart.

They are patterned after various kinds of secular organizations.

They have no gospel or theological convictions.

They do not have a mission outside the church and do not consider lost people.

They do not take into account any surrounding cultural engagement.

They are simply arguing over leading from the top down through authority or from the bottom up through service.

They bog down from either too much hierarchy or too little leadership.

They are static organizational structures that are not moving on a mission.

Seeking a better alternative, I then read Rick Warren's book *The Purpose-Driven Church*, which has become one of the most popular books ever written for pastors.[15] In this book, Warren teaches an entirely new way to organize a church, which is illustrated on the next page.

In the Purpose-Driven ecclesiology, the goal is to move as many people as possible into leadership at the center of the church. This is accomplished by having various classes to train people for ministry and to prepare them to become more vitally invested in the church. The Purpose-Driven model had some of the same flaws as the other models, with four major positive exceptions: (1) It moved Christians in the church from being customers served by their pastor to being ministers serving according to their spiritual gifts. (2) It shifted the duty of the pastor(s) from doing ministry for Christians to training Christians to do the ministry, as Ephesians 4:11 – 13 teaches. (3) It finally put lost people on the church organizational chart and had the church existing for them and not just for the Christians already in the church. (4) It put the mission of evangelism at the forefront of the church.

The changes brought about by Warren are revolutionary and very important. His ecclesiology has become the standard for the contemporary and evangelical church. God has used Warren's insights to bring untold numbers of people to Jesus, and Warren has become one of the most important Christians in our generation. Sadly, there was a time when, as an arrogant young punk, I was critical of his work. But after connecting with Warren a few times, I have found him to be a good man who loves Jesus, works hard, and is just trying to make a difference. If anyone buys my book, maybe some young punk will talk trash about me in a few years, and then I'll know I've done something important enough to be criticized too. So I appreciate Warren's contribution to the larger church and

Purpose-Driven Ecclesiology

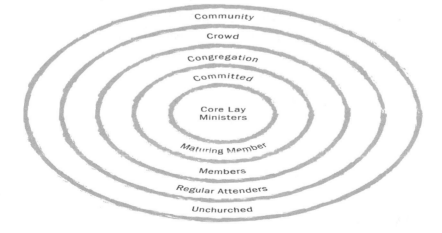

believe his work is the most effective church growth strategy for the kind of people who are best reached by the contemporary and evangelical church.

As I continued to study, however, I did not believe that any of the ecclesiological options that I studied would be the most effective structure for the mission of an urban emerging and evangelical church like ours. God clearly spoke to me as a new Christian and told me to plant a church in Seattle that focused on reaching young men. But Seattle is among the least likely cities in the nation where a young man would attend church. It was obvious that they would not simply come to church on their own and that if we truly wanted to grow, we would need to be structured differently than all of the churches in the city who had not successfully reached young, creative, and urban secular men.

Around this time, I became acquainted with the Gospel and Our Culture Network (GOCN).[16] This network is a denominational think tank of sorts wrestling with what it means to do missions in America. One of the leaders, Dr. George Hunsberger, taught at a conference we hosted in Seattle for Leadership Network. About one hundred young pastors and leaders attended, and his insights were very helpful. I also met another member of the GOCN, Alan Roxburgh, who is a really good thinker from Canada. In a few pages of one of his books, he articulates many of the concerns about church structures that I shared above and provides the beginnings of an alternative.[17] I began wrestling with his basic concept and came up with the following emerging and missional ecclesiology, which has governed our church ever since.

Emerging and Missional Ecclesiology

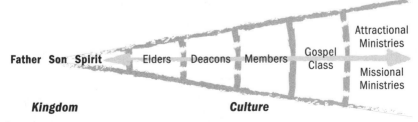

The emerging and missional ecclesiology has the following elements:

The Trinitarian God is the source and model of loving community.

The Trinitarian God rules over the church and culture as Lord over all so that ministry extends far beyond the church and into culture.

Jesus mediates between the church on earth and God the Father in heaven.

Jesus is the Senior Pastor to be followed by the power of the Holy Spirit.

The church has two simultaneous missions: going out into culture (missional ministry) and bringing people into God's kingdom, of which the church is an outpost (attractional ministry).

A clear gospel thread binds everyone and everything together on Jesus' mission.

The structure is rooted in biblical theology, not secular organizational theory.

The church exists to welcome and convert lost people.

The church labors to be as culturally accessible to lost people as possible.

The church has leaders but is not organized by hierarchy.

Elders are a qualified team of male pastors who are player-coaches both leading the church and training people for ministry.

Deacons are qualified male and female pastoral associates.

Members are church leaders who give their money, service, prayers, and time to the advancement of the gospel and submit to discipline if needed.

The Gospel Class is the filter through which the wrong people are weeded out of the church and the right people are welcomed into the church as members.

As I became convinced that the ecclesiological structure I had settled on was biblical, I then implemented it. The details of that process will require another book, so here I will simply hit the main points.

As Jesus did when selecting his disciples, I started by prayerfully asking God the Father which men he wanted to be chosen as leaders. I then sought out men who had expressed a desire to become elders, were already functioning as pastors in the church, and met the biblical criteria. I also looked up their financial giving to the church because Jesus taught that our money follows our heart, and I wanted to see if these men were truly with me on the mission to build our church. It was encouraging to see that each of these men was giving more time and more money to the church than anyone else gave, because they loved the Lord and our church as much as anyone else we had.

We began meeting together in a weekly Bible study. We studied the Pastoral Epistles (1 and 2 Timothy, Titus) as well as some other books that were assigned reading. As we studied, it became clear that these men would be a good team. Practically, I considered them peers and the kind of men that I hoped one day my sons would become and my daughters would marry. Additionally, by getting to know their wives and families well, I was convinced that they were the kind of families that I wanted to be the examples in our church for others to emulate, as Hebrews 13:7 teaches.

I also did a great deal of biblical and historical research on women in ministry. Again, the findings could fill an entire book, but to keep things brief, I will simply lean over the plate and take one for my team that, like Jesus did, only appoints men to the highest position of spiritual leadership. After hundreds of hours of study, I felt convinced that a complementarian position was the most biblical, as the following chart illustrates.[18]

As the elder candidates finished their training and testing process, I preached a series on how we were going to organize our church. One Sunday I brought our first elder team before the church to officially install them as pastors. Since we are an independent

Egalitarian (liberal)	Complementarian (moderate)	Hierarchical (conservative)
Men and women are partners together in every arena of ministry. All ministries and offices in the church are open to all qualified men and women. Gender does not exclude any person from any church office.	All church ministries are open to qualified men and women, with the singular exception of elder-pastor, which is only open to qualified men. Women can be deacons, teach, lead worship, serve communion, and be in full-time paid ministry.	Women and men are created to operate in different spheres of church ministry. Women cannot be elders or deacons, serve communion, teach men, lead worship, or speak in the church service. Women can only build ministries for women and children.
Priority texts: Judges 4; Acts 16:11–15; 18:26; Luke 8:1–3; Romans 16:1–3, 6–7, 12; Galatians 3:28	**Priority texts:** Same as hierarchical, with an emphasis on 1 Timothy 3:11 and Romans 16:1–2	**Priority texts:** Genesis 1:27; 2:18; 3:16–17; 1 Corinthians 11:3, 8–9; 1 Timothy 2:11–3:13

church, we also ordained each of the seven men (including myself), with our church serving as the licensing organization, kind of like the scene in the movie *The Apostle* where Robert Duvall, who plays the role of the pastor, baptizes himself as an apostle.

The elders were a great assistance to me because they picked up a lot of the pastoral work, such as leading small groups, teaching classes, counseling, and developing leaders. The elders put in enough time that it was equivalent to having at least two more full-time pastors on staff. This allowed me to pull back a bit from working in the church and spend more time working on the church. Because the giving was still poor, I was the only paid pastor on staff, and most of my income still came from outside the church.

With elders in place, I could focus on building church membership. This was absolutely essential to our survival since people had come into the church with different agendas, theological convictions, levels of commitment, and missions. I needed to create a filter to get the wrong people out of the church and keep the right people in the church. I then needed to explain to our people what they needed to do for our church to stay on mission. So I developed a class that has had a few names over the years but is now called the Gospel Class.

The Gospel Class is a series of Bible studies that I taught to ground our people in our essential doctrines and missiology, much of which is included in this book. I did not want anyone to hold a leadership position, teach, join a small group, or receive any training in a class until they had first completed the Gospel Class and signed a covenant agreement with the elders that was very serious and demanded a lot from the church members. Though it may sound harsh, I did not want our church to invest time and energy into people who were not on our mission.

The first incarnation of the Gospel Class met in my home, and I taught all of the lessons to about a dozen people. Before long, one of the other elders was also teaching a class of about a dozen people in his home. As people completed the class, they were encouraged to either sign up as members or leave the church and go elsewhere. I wanted a church filled with missionaries, Christians who were learning how to become missionaries, and lost people. I would not accept a church filled with Christians who did not give, serve, or reach lost people, because they invariably make themselves and their selfish desires the mission of a church and kill innovation and momentum.

From its inception, anywhere from one-quarter to one-half of the people who begin the Gospel Class each quarter do not become members, for reasons ranging from doctrinal differences to not wanting to meet our membership demands. The class has run every quarter since it began.

Once we had members, the elders then began tracking their financial giving twice a year to ensure that our members were supporting their church. I was horrified to discover that most of the people I had previously considered committed had not been giving anything until they became members. Even more horrifying was learning this about the richest person in our church, who was making a few hundred thousand dollars a year and who was also one of the most vocal and visible people in the church. This person had given only a few hundred dollars the previous year. Conversely, a high school girl who worked part-time at an ice-cream shop had given more money than this person who wanted to be a leader over her.

Our people were generally very young and very poor. I knew that unless everyone gave, we would never make ends meet because we did not have a sugar daddy to bail us out. So we started asking members for annual giving pledges, tracked their giving, and contacted them if their giving was significantly below their pledge.[19] Our attitude in making the calls was not accusatory but rather inquisitive. The elders who made the calls simply asked if everything was okay, assuming that the members who were not giving had a viable reason. Most of them said that they had lost a job or had been hit with an unforeseen major expense such as a medical crisis, so we ended up praying for them and giving out benevolence support to those in need. For those who were just sinning by not giving, we asked them to kindly do their part, and they did.

Once the members were in place, we then began holding home Bible studies and theology classes for training and had a more faithful base of people serving. In general, people stepped up and took ownership of our church and its mission. The financial giving improved enough that I was able to start supporting my family with only my church salary as my outside support dried up. We improved our sound equipment and got some computers and telephones to expand the office at the church we were renting.

We then put unpaid deacons in place, who began building new ministries. The deacons reorganized the children's ministry and church service details, provided meals for new moms, held bridal showers and baby showers, began a prayer ministry, and created a nice updated website.

Our two services were filling up as our attendance climbed to more than three hundred people, and it felt like things were finally maturing and coming together, just in time to fall apart again.

Reformission Reflections

1. Does the community surrounding your church or ministry view you warmly or coldly? Why?

2. How well does your church or ministry take care of the pastor and his family? Are they paid well, respected, and encouraged? Is there anything else that should be done for them?

3. On a scale of 1 to 10, with 1 being poor and 10 being excellent, how well are people learning about Jesus from the Bible through the preaching and teaching in your church or ministry?

4. Is your church or ministry led more like a congregational, senior pastor, Purpose-Driven, or emerging and missional ministry?

5. Are you personally in favor of an egalitarian, complementarian, or hierchical view of women in ministry? What verses from Scripture do you have to support your position?

6. Is your church or ministry in favor of an egalitarian, complementarian, or hierarchical view of women in ministry?

CHAPTER FIVE

I was not a Christian when
I came to the church.

Today I am a pastor.

Jesus, Why Am I Getting Fatter and Meaner?

350 – 1,000 People

It was not a happy time. It was the fall of 1999, just after the shootings at Columbine High School and just before Americans were spinning like tops over the end of the world, which was supposed to be brought on by the Y2K bug. Thankfully, Seattle grunge had nearly run its course, and the local thrift stores were filled with used flannel shirts and boots. Tragically, grunge was replaced with happy-clappy, half-naked teenage girls, like Christina Aguilera and Britney Spears, and boy bands that danced and still had the audacity to claim they were heterosexual. More than Y2K, it was the rise of the teeny-bop pop that caused me to think the end of the world might indeed be imminent.

Our little church was rolling along rather nicely. We had settled into our rented church and had grown to nearly 350 people a week. In fall, I started preaching through the book of Exodus. We also changed our worship service to include communion every week and put most of the congregational singing after the sermon as a response to the hearing of God's Word through the preaching. We felt free to do so because no commanded order of a church service is to be found anywhere in Scripture, nor is any detailed example of a worship service from the first-century church. Scripture nowhere requires a fixed order for church services but simply teaches that things should be done in a way that is "fitting and orderly" and that reveres God (1 Cor. 14:40; Heb. 12:28).

Churches services commonly last approximately one hour or less. Churches wanting to have short services must therefore choose between singing songs, partaking of communion, praying, and preaching. Most churches virtually, if not entirely, omit at least one of these four major aspects of worship for the sake of time. Mars Hill began with only a few songs, a sermon, and monthly communion but over the years has grown to include each of the four major aspects of a worship service. Because of this, our worship service takes up to two hours and is an event that people simply make time for, not unlike a big concert or movie. We made the sermon the hinge for the service, with time for repentance, giving, communion, and most of the congregational singing following the sermon to provide people an opportunity to process God's Word and respond to his initiation in their lives.

It felt good to be making progress and to settle into a groove with good momentum. We were forming our own identity, people were coming to faith in Jesus, young people were getting married, babies were being born, our financial state was climbing out of the toilet, and for the first time in our church history, I was actually feeling happy and hopeful.

Then came *that* Monday.

On *that* Monday, I was told via letter that the building had been sold and some other church was evicting us, effective immediately. We had only days to leave the premises and take all of our things with us. I can still remember reading the letter over and over in utter disbelief.

We lost our offices.

We lost our worship space.

We lost our midweek class space.

We lost our band practice space.

We had nowhere to meet for church services the following week.

We had no idea where we would go or what we would do.

To make matters worse, our office had been broken into and our computer with our database was stolen the week before we were evicted. We could not even notify our people, via phone, mail, or email, that we were homeless.

And the new building owner kicked us out of our office, which meant we had no phone for people to even call us to find out where we were moving to. Amidst our move, the phone company went on strike, and it was over a month before we had a phone number of any kind. Our church simply vanished without a trace.

On Tuesday I still had no idea where we were going to meet for church the following Sunday. I had twenty-four hours to find a new place to meet because I was scheduled to leave town on Wednesday to speak at a conference out of state. In desperation, I attended my first citywide pastors' meeting, which a large church downtown was hosting. Every pastor at the meeting was at least as old as my dad, and most were wearing suits that did not really fit well around the middle. I anticipated this and intentionally wore a shirt with buttons and tried to just stay quiet in hopes that they would think I was legit. Eventually they asked for prayer requests, and I said I needed one of them to let me use their building on Sunday nights for an indefinite period of time at no charge, beginning in five days.

The pastor hosting the meeting kindly offered to let us use his church for free on Sunday nights. He then walked me into the sanctuary. The room sat over one thousand people. It was so big that we would fit in it like a toddler fits in his father's clothing. The acoustics worked well for a choir but were death for a hard-rock worship team. The building was at least thirty minutes from our old location, in the middle of downtown, and was surrounded by panhandlers and drunks, who peed on the church. We took the pastor up on his offer because it was better than meeting outside in a park in the rain, which was our only other option.

I asked our key leaders to call everyone they knew and tell them about the move. We put signs on the door of the building we had vacated and left a few guys there to hand out directions to people who showed up and hoped for the best. I boarded a plane on Wednesday to go speak at a conference and was gone until the following week.

We cancelled the 7:00 p.m. service and rolled back to one service at 5:00 p.m. Lief preached the first Sunday, and it was rough because we were not ready to pull off child care, sound, worship, and all the details. We had to cancel all of our midweek programming, the church went into survival mode, and our attendance dropped noticeably.

The whole mess really bummed me out. One particularly low point was the Sunday when a drunken lady in a dirty T-shirt wandered down the long center aisle as I was preaching to yell at me for stealing land from the Indians, demanding that I give it back. I tried to explain to her that she had the wrong white guy because I rented a house, did not own any land, and was sorry about the Indians. But she was not dissuaded. Lief escorted her out and was so kind that she tried to make out with him.

At this point, we had been in four locations, had held services at four different times, and had had six phone numbers in a few years. I had worked myself to near burnout and was still the only paid pastor on staff although there was enough work for ten people.

To make matters worse, I was not even certain that I would pastor Mars Hill for a long time. My plan had been to start the church and possibly hand it off to one of the elders and move on and plant another church. It was pretty devastating after a few years of hard work to be back to a core group under two hundred and starting over.

I remember going for a walk one day along Lake Washington, which was near my house. I stopped and stared at the ground for about an hour, running through my options in my mind, trying to figure out what to do, and feeling like a caged animal. Should I shut down the church? Should I contact one of the other churches in the area and come in as a church-within-a-church service for them? Should I jump ship and let Lief or Mike figure it out? Should I hang in there and either turn things around or die trying?

I loved the elders and the members in the church who were willing to hang in with me no matter what happened. And I felt obligated to do everything in my power to fight for the mission Jesus had called me to and I had called them to. I vividly remember the day shortly thereafter when I stood before what was left of my church and told my people that I was giving them my life. I was going to buy a home, plant my flag in the ground, and give the rest of my life to them, our city, and our mission. I promised them that we would succeed or I would literally die trying and begged them to do the same.

A friend in the church kindly allowed me to move into a large home he owned on a lease-to-own deal because I was too broke to qualify to buy anything beyond an outhouse. The seventy-year-old house had over three thousand square feet, seven bedrooms on three floors, and needed a ton of work because it had been neglected for many years as a rental home for college students. Grace and I and our daughter Ashley, three male renters who helped cover the mortgage, my study, and the church office all moved into the home. This put me on the job, literally, twenty-four hours a day, seven days a week, as the boundary between home and church was erased.

We ran the church out of my house for nearly two years, including leadership meetings and Bible studies for various groups on almost every night of the week. It was not uncommon to have over seventy people a week in our home. Grace got sucked right back into the church mess. She was a great host to our guests. But I started getting bitter toward her because I was again feeling neglected.

I began working seven days a week, trying to save the church from imminent death. I had decided to go for broke and accepted that I would either save the church and provide for my family or probably die of a heart attack. I lived on caffeine and adrenaline for the better part of two years, ate terribly, and put on nearly forty pounds.

To reorganize the church, we also started two intentional living communities in large homes near mine. One became a men's ministry home called the White Horse Inn, named after the pub Martin Luther frequented. The other became a women's home called Noonday, named after a verse in Isaiah. Both homes housed around ten people and were used to build Christian community, host Bible studies, dinner parties, lectures, and serve along with my home as the relational and ministry centers of the church.

During this time, I also saw an increase in spiritual attacks. A number of people started scheduling meetings with me to explain horrific demonic attacks they were experiencing. I also started getting a number of prophetic dreams from God to help me make important decisions that saved our church.

Additionally, I started getting random words of knowledge. The first I ever got came years prior while I was hosting the radio program because Lief was on vacation. A man I had never spoken to before called in from the Midwest to complain about the state of American Christianity and proceeded to rip into the hypocrisy in his own church. I rebuked him for committing adultery on his wife and said he hated his church because he came under conviction there for being an adulterer, and unless he dumped his girlfriend and repented to his wife, God would deal severely with him. I can still remember just staring at the microphone in front of my face, wanting to take back the words that I had just sent out around the country. There was a long silence, and then the man broke down and confessed my words as truth.

Up to this point, I had been basically a theological cessationist and a fan of fundamentalist straw-man attacks on charismatic Christians. It wasn't until some years later, however, that I came to see the cessationists' interpretation of 1 Corinthians 12 – 14 as the second worst exegesis I have ever read, next to that of a Canadian nudist arsonist cult I once did some research on.

I also had not really believed in Satan or demons, spiritual warfare, or the use of certain spiritual gifts with more than a head knowledge that essentially ignored these things as part of my ministry. Now I was operating for the first time in my life with spiritual power, insight, and authority. For example, one day a woman from the church walked by me, and God told me that she had been physically abused by her husband the night before. So I stopped her and asked her if her husband had beaten her the night before and forbid her from telling anyone. Immediately she broke down and confessed what had happened.

My family also started coming under spiritual attack. At one point, my daughter Ashley, who was only a few years old, started having a really bad attitude. Despite days of repeated discipline, her behavior did not improve, and I was befuddled as to why. Late one night I went in to check on her, and she was still awake. I asked her why she was not sleeping, and she began to cry but refused to tell me. I prayed over her, and eventually she told me that for days she had not slept much because "bad angels" kept showing up in her room, saying bad things about Jesus and pulling her hair when she tried to sleep. They scared her by saying that if she told me, they would kill me. She had been acting up for a few days because she was sleep deprived, and I had been disciplining her sternly because I was worn out and on edge. I broke down and wept openly for the first time I can remember in my adult life and held my daughter, praying over her and repenting to God for allowing the Enemy to drive a wedge between my daughter and me.

It was clear that I needed to better understand the supernatural and demonic side of ministry. So I spent a few months reading every book I could find on Satan, demons, and spiritual warfare.[1] I met with older pastors who were wise in these areas. I also studied every occurrence of this issue in the Bible, trying to get a handle on what I was up against and how I was supposed to respond.

Through study and prayer, I started to better understand the schemes of Satan and demons and how to help liberate people from spiritual oppression with the principles of Ephesians 6:10–20. By God's liberating power, many people stopped taking medications because the tormenting voices and panic attacks went away. Some people were also miraculously healed. I did not speak much about these things because I feared they would detract from our focus on Jesus and that our young people would start to see me as a guru, which I did not want. But I was grateful to be able to help these people I loved, and that part of my ministry quietly continues to this day.

During this difficult season, I was burned-out, overworked, out of shape, stressed, and had picked up a nervous twitch in my eye along with ongoing acid reflux and high blood pressure. I was not sleeping much, and my sleep was often interrupted due to stress that kept me awake, thinking. I would also often wake up after a prophetic dream or spiritual attack to pray strategically, which only contributed to the fatigue. But thanks to growing insights on how to win spiritual battles, I was optimistic that we would weather the storm and that the church would survive.

Then I had the worst experience of my whole life.

I went to bed one night hoping to get caught up on sleep. In the middle of the night, I had a prophetic type of dream that was like other prophetic dreams I had previously except it did not include Scripture that clarified its meaning, because it was from Satan. I cannot go into great detail about the dream because it would impugn the character of someone else. Something horrendous happened to this person that I was not present to witness. But my dream was the equivalent of a horrifying film that showed me every gruesome detail of the worst day of their life. I was not present for the sin they committed, but I told them about my dream later and they confirmed the very graphic details that I saw.

The dream was so vivid that I felt sick and woke up just in time to run into the bathroom and throw up in the toilet. I went downstairs and spent the rest of the night sitting on the couch, staring blankly into the dark and asking God to allow me to do anything but be a pastor. I just wanted to be done with ministry and do something, anything, that would not kill me before I turned thirty.

For weeks, I watched the mental film every night as I tried to sleep. I knew it was an accusation but could not get it to stop, and so the torment continued night after night (Rev. 12:10b). Not knowing what to do, I withdrew from God and my wife and threw myself into my work to keep my mind occupied with something else. I sometimes worked all night just so that I would not have to go to bed and watch the nightmare yet again.

During this time, I was also frantically searching for a home for our church. We were treading water, but it was obvious that we could not last for much longer in our temporary location. And

I desperately needed to get the church office, secretary, and all meetings out of my home. I spent hundreds of hours looking at every option I could think of, without even one possibility surfacing because space was limited and we were poor.

Then I called an older man, Stan, who was serving as a consultant for a dying church that I had heard about. He explained that only a handful of elderly people remained in a small church building on the other side of town, and he had been brought in to recommend what they should do since they had no pastor and no future. I asked him to give the building to our struggling church for free. He was a very godly older man who agreed to try, which dropped a bit of rain amidst our hope drought.

I started attending the weekly prayer meeting of this small church, which consisted of a handful of women in their eighties, one "young" woman in her sixties, and one elderly man. I also occasionally preached on Sunday mornings for the less than ten of them from a King James Bible while wearing a suit.

Eventually, they voted—to give the church to a Chinese church instead of us.

I was absolutely devastated. Then a few weeks later, I got a call from Stan, who said that the Chinese church had inexplicably declined the offer and did not want the free building. So, like Abraham receiving the Promised Land from Lot, we got the building!

The building was in bad shape. The older congregation had not been downstairs much over the years, and the old Sunday school rooms were full of junk. One of the heaters was broken, and the wiring was so old it was not even grounded and, therefore, could not be used for computers. The flooring was old asbestos tile. And the walls were mostly a smurfy shade of blue. It would take a lot of money and months of work to make the place functional since it was cutting-edge in about 1923.

During the negotiations for the building, we had also pursued another meeting location. The oldest theater in Seattle, called "the Ave," near the University of Washington on the main drag, had come up for sale. We had been eyeing the vacant and dilapidated small property for years. Lief had quickly put an offer on the place and got it.

We had a ton of work to do to make the space useable for church services and all-ages rock concerts. The roof leaked, the place was filled with junk, the seats were musty and broken, and rat poop was everywhere. We knew we could never run all of our church services out of the theater because it was too small for offices, classes, or kids' space. But it was a strategic location for Sunday church services and for concerts throughout the week to reach college students and the young panhandling homeless kids.

To better coordinate the volunteers working on the project, we got an office across the street from the theater, which we had renamed "The Paradox." But all we could afford was an upstairs apartment in a condemned building. The main floor of our building was a former ghetto East Indian grocery that was vacant and filled with rats and homeless kids. The basement was a favorite hangout for local junkies who did black-tar heroin — the area is one of the nation's most saturated black-tar heroin trafficking areas. A few years later Layne Staley, from the band Alice in Chains, died of a heroin overdose nearby.

We never paid for electricity in our office apartment because the building was illegally hooked up to the power grid and all our power was stolen. We did, however, have a high phone bill. Though the slumlord denied it, he often keyed into our office in the middle of the night to make lengthy phone calls to India.

The back of the Paradox was a favorite spot for local junkies to shoot up drugs and poop on the ground. Brad and Eric, who had both recently come on staff with small salaries, called me one morning to leave a peculiar voicemail. They had shown up that morning to work on the building and spotted a homeless junkie sleeping on the back steps. They yelled at him and he did not wake up. They approached him and shook him, but he still did not wake up. Because he was dead. On our church steps.

Rather than calling the cops or an ambulance, Eric and Brad first called me to hurry up and come see the dead guy. I did not get the voicemail in time. So eventually they called the cops, who brought out the coroner to haul the dead junkie away.

Suddenly we had gone from being homeless to being a church with two buildings. The only problems were that the buildings were about twenty minutes apart and both needed a lot of renovation, which required money that we did not have. Lief was kind enough to do most of the major work on the Paradox with his construction company, along with the volunteers who worked hard to get the building ready for occupancy.

One humble and godly couple in the church came into some money and asked me to meet them for coffee. During our meeting, they told me they wanted to give $200,000 to pay for the renovations on the buildings we had gotten. I nearly died; it was about $198,000 more than the largest check we had ever cashed previously.

Their money, along with much smaller gifts from people in the church, allowed us to renovate both the church building and the Paradox at the same time. Both facilities were finished around the same time, and we moved the offices to the church building and began hosting concerts at the Paradox.

I was far more excited about the Paradox than about the old church. The old church had a horrendous location, hidden in an old neighborhood far away from any major freeway, which made it as hard to find as a fundamentalist having fun. My only hope for the building was to use it for offices and midweek classes and meetings.

Conversely, the Paradox was a great opportunity to be in a hip neighborhood with the only exclusively all-ages concert venue in the city, thanks to a legal loophole we exploited. The Paradox only rarely hosted Christian bands since our main goal was getting non-Christian kids to come to the concerts. Our focus was hospitality. Paul commanded the church at Rome to practice hospitality, and one the qualifications for elders-pastors is that they practice hospitality. Many Christians wrongly think that hospitality is the welcoming of fellow Christians into their home and church for friendship. But that is fellowship. Hospitality is when Christians welcome strangers, especially non-Christians, into their homes, lives, and church. So we welcomed kids into a safe place where we could build relationships of grace on Jesus' behalf rather than preaching at the kids or doing goofy things like handing out tracts.

In its first few years, the Paradox hosted about 650 concerts for about 65,000 kids. We have had only a few minor problems, like the Japanese punk band that got naked during their set for no apparent reason and another band that set off fireworks during their show. The Paradox has seen many kids come to faith through relationships and has helped us maintain a very good relationship with the music and alternative-life scene in Seattle because we genuinely love the kids who are into punk, hardcore, and indie rock.

The 5:00 p.m. service remained in the big church downtown, and we started a new service at 7:00 p.m. in the Paradox. I drove between the two to preach. At the first Paradox service, Team Strikeforce led worship and I preached to the thirty or forty kids who showed up.

We also needed to start a morning service in the old church building because we had promised the elderly folks who gave us the building that we would. I got stuck preaching that service because none of the elders would. Assuming the morning service at the old church building was a waste of time, I asked the church secretary to help me launch the morning service and did not bring any other leaders with me.

The first week of having three services in three locations was disappointing because the two new services were very small, while the evening service downtown was holding steady at a few hundred people. I was hoping that at least one of the sites would get traction and grow, but it did seem silly to have three services for about 250 people in three buildings with a combined seating of more than 1,400.

To make matters worse, I took my first overseas trip to train a number of pastors in India. The first leg of the flight took all night, and I barely slept because I was in a middle seat on a packed flight and my head bobbed around all night like a buoy on a lake. We had a layover in an Asian country, and in the airport was a nice hotel with a spa. I decided to go in for a massage to get the knots out of my neck before the next lengthy flight and then take a shower, brush my teeth, and change my clothes. The attractive woman performing the massage was hot — like hell. I was nearly asleep during the massage, until the moment she kindly asked me if I wanted any sexual favors and began to list her impressive skills.

This was not good.

I was burned-out, underpaid, in debt, sexually frustrated due to an unspectacular sex life, under frequent demonic attack, and so stressed that my blood pressure hovered somewhere between heart-attack victim and mulch in the ground, and now found myself alone with an attractive woman in a foreign country. In retrospect, I think the decision I made in that moment was perhaps the most significant ministry decision I have ever made. To be honest, I was incredibly tempted. I closed my eyes and took a deep breath, trying to figure out what my answer was. In my mind I saw Joseph running from Potiphar's wife.

So I jumped up from the massage table like a kid with a bee sting, grabbed my things in one hand, and ran out of the room, down the hallway, and out of the hotel. I vowed to God that I would get my life under control upon returning home. That day was my proverbial fork in the road, and I shudder to think that had I chosen sin, our church and my marriage would likely not be intact today.

Shortly after returning home a few weeks later, I absolutely cracked. In one day I had around ten hours of back-to-back meetings with young single men in the church, which pushed me over the edge. Every one of them was older than me, a chronic masturbator, a porn addict, banging weak-willed girls like a screen door in a stiff breeze, not tithing, and wanting me to hang out with them a lot to keep them accountable. By about the fourth or fifth guy, something in me completely snapped. I stood up and cussed out the poor guy, losing my mind to the point that I think I actually cuffed him upside the head. I told him that in Galatians 6:1–5 we are told that guys need to take care of light burdens and only burden the church with big issues and that guys older than me would need to get their erections under control because it was not my job.

It then dawned on me that I was dealing with an imbecile epidemic. Most of our guys never had a dad and were either cowardly mama's boys or thuggish pervert jerks. The problem was that neither type was sufficient for building a church that could reach the city for Jesus. Worse still, seemingly every guy in the church was a slave to his lusts. Frightfully, only a few weeks earlier, I had nearly taken Satan's bait myself without seeing the hook.

At this time, our church also started an unmoderated discussion board on our website, called Midrash, and it was being inundated with postings by emerging-church-type feminists and liberals. I went onto the site and posted as William Wallace II, after the great Scottish man portrayed in the movie *Braveheart*, and attacked those who were posting. It got insane, and thousands of posts were being made each day until it was discovered that it was me raging like a madman under the guise of a movie character. One guy got so mad that he actually showed up at my house to fight me one night around 3:00 a.m.

Things were starting to get out of hand with the men, so I called a meeting and demanded that all of the men in our church attend. I preached for more than two hours about manhood and basically gave the dad talk to my men for looking at porno, sleeping with young women, not serving Christ, not working hard at their jobs, and so on. I demanded that the men who were with me on our mission to change the city stay and that the rest leave the church and stop getting in the way because you can't charge hell with your pants around your ankles, a bottle of lotion in one hand, and a Kleenex in the other.

On their way out of that meeting, I handed each man two stones and told them that on this day God was giving them their balls back to get the courage to do kingdom work. Guys put them on their monitors at work or glued them to the dash of their truck and kept them like stones of remembrance from the Old Testament. The next week the offering doubled and the men caught fire. It was a surreal time, since I was basically fathering guys my own age and treating them more like a military unit than a church.

The life change was unreal. We had guys getting saved en masse. We had gay guys going straight. We had guys tossing out porn, getting jobs, tithing, taking wives, buying homes, making babies, and repenting of the sins of their fathers. We had guys who had divorced their wives remarrying them. We had men adopting children so they would have a Christian father. It was a lot like Acts because the whole city seemed to be abuzz.

This season was messy and I sinned and cussed a lot, but God somehow drew a straight line with my crooked Philistine stick. I had a good mission, but some of my tactics were born out of anger and burnout, and I did a lot of harm and damage while attracting a lot of attention. I was justifiably angry, but did not faithfully heed Paul's command not to let anger lead me into sin (Eph. 4:26).

Some of the fired-up young guys went too far and started acting like young bucks in rutting season, wanting to lock horns with me and the elders. Many went into extreme forms of Calvinism and wanted to debate things like theonomy and other dumb things that only white guys with high-speed Internet connections to bizarre websites could get into and were causing division. If you don't know what theonomy is, don't worry, because you aren't really missing anything. Basically, it is the belief that the church should rule the world, including the banking system, government, and so on, and enforce Old Testament law like Israel did. The young rabid Calvinists who were pushing for this doctrine did not yet own homes, most did not even have wives, and some still lived with their mothers. I tried to set them straight by telling them to get dominion over their room before they took over the world, but like most fools, they were not deterred.

There were too many guys to fight individually, and I needed a way to fight with them all at once. So in an effort to clean up the mess, I started a weekly men-only meeting, which I named "Dead Men" and which ran for a few months. I paired guys up to debate an assigned theological issue, and other guys in the audience would chuck things at them and mock them if their study was not good or their argument not cogent. At the end of the debate, we would vote, declare a winner, and give him a mock prize and crown him with a Viking helmet. The men liked the competition and got into studying and debating theology.

When the hyper-Calvinists realized we weren't going to baptize their babies or talk about stupid stuff that detracts from mission, many of them left, which was a good thing because they were getting to be deadweight. Over the years, I've just accepted that if I do not quickly open the back door when God is trying to run people out of our church, I am working against God by keeping sick people in my church so that they can infect others. Indeed, the church is a body, and one of the most important parts is the colon. Like the human body, any church body without a colon is destined for sickness that leads to death.

During this melee, a nearby Christian college whose students are mostly female and feminist had a few guys ask me to come and speak to their dorm floor about masculinity. A buzz went out on campus, and perhaps a few hundred guys showed up. We debated manhood until after midnight, and I was soon banned from coming back to the campus again, which only added to the buzz. These Christian "guys" were so effeminate it was unbelievable. In the end, I unnecessarily burned the bridge at the college in a public debate with the head of the theology department before hundreds of students on the issue of ministers in skirts. I'm pretty sure I won the debate while losing a warm relationship with the college, which was likely unwise.

We also began "boot camps" for our young men, teaching them how to get a wife, have sex with that wife, get a job, budget money, buy a house, father a child, study the Bible, stop looking at porn, and brew decent beer. The buzz hit just as we opened the 7:00 p.m. Paradox service and the 10:00 a.m. service at the small church building, in addition to the 5:00 p.m. downtown service. I chose to preach on the most controversial practical life issues, such as dating, gender, work, kids, sex, money, and the like, in a long topical series from the book of Proverbs to continue fanning the fire that was burning in our church among the young men who had caught the vision to become patriarchs.

Both locations took off at the same time solely through word of mouth. The two hundred Paradox seats filled up in less than a year, and we went to 6:00 p.m. and 8:00 p.m. services in addition to the 5:00 p.m. service downtown. Though the 10:00 a.m. service in the small church building started with forty people and no fanfare, it exploded like a bomb. We learned that unchurched people tend to be the most traditional when it comes to church. For years, we had held services only on Sunday nights trying to be cool, different, and therefore more attractive to unchurched people. But our first morning service took off in part because unchurched people thought that church was an event that happened in a church building on a Sunday morning.

People kept coming solely through word of mouth, and we kept adding services. Within a year, the original 10:00 a.m. service in the new church building became three morning services (9:00 a.m., 11:00 a.m., and 1:00 p.m.), in addition to the existing 5:00 p.m. service, which we moved from downtown into the small church building. The small church room only seated about 180 people, but within a year, the services there exploded from 40 to about 800 people. People were jammed in throughout the building, and we put speakers in the basement, around corners, and in offices so that people could at least listen to the sermon though they could not see me or the band. Some Sundays we had to leave the doors open and have the single men stand outside with coats on during the service because we could not physically pack another person into the church. We had only one toilet for each gender and only one parking spot, and Sundays were a mayhem marathon.

The longest sermon I preached was about an hour and forty minutes, without any notes, and one church service would often last so long that it still would not be done when the next service was supposed to be beginning. I was on such a rampage that I really did not care about the clock and just kept ranting until I had said everything I wanted to say. During this time, I finally learned how to preach with consistency week in and week out. Though preaching for six to nine hours on Sundays nearly killed me, it also helped me refine each sermon by improving on it each of the six times I preached it, after getting feedback and answering questions from people after each sermon. Simply, preaching is like driving a clutch, and the only way to figure it out is to keep grinding the gears and stalling until you figure it out.

The sermons were so long that we really did not have any breaks between services and just kept singing and preaching all day. People came in and out whenever they liked and stuck around long enough to sing, hear one sermon, and take communion. It was an absolute logistical nightmare, but the buzz just kept growing so that people started showing up over an hour early to reserve a seat for themselves and their friends. It was peculiar to look out before our 5:00 p.m. evening service and see people eating dinner an hour before the service began to ensure they could get a good seat in our small church.

Parking was so scarce that people walked for many blocks to get to the church, and the neighbors started complaining because we had once again completely overtaken a previously nice, quiet neighborhood. The fire marshal was sent out to shut us down but got saved, which bought us some time. Many of the neighbors came to the church, and some came to Christ.

Next door to our church lived a very large, very loud, and very unpleasant woman. She went to another local church and often walked into our services to publicly cuss us all out. I nicknamed her "the finger lady" because she often sat on her front porch giving our people the finger and calling them whores and bastards while they walked to the church, as she chain-smoked and perfected her self-induced Tourette's syndrome. We never forbade her from coming in to interrupt our services, and her insanity only added to our buzz since everyone talked about the church with the crazy big lady who periodically waddled in to cuss people out during the service.

During this time, I was suffering from vertigo. I had taught at a conference on a cruise ship, and something got messed up in my inner ear. I spent the year feeling incredibly dizzy because of a strange syndrome that usually happens only to middle-aged menopausal women after a cruise. It was not the kind of manly diagnosis I was hoping for, such as being dizzy because I had too much testosterone in my body. The dizziness got so bad that one day while tilting my head to look at a video on a lower shelf in a store, I actually fell over like a drunk. Driving a car became a harrowing adventure not unlike drinking and driving because my depth perception was completely off.

Nonetheless, I was preaching upward of an hour and a half six times a day and driving between two buildings with constant dizziness. Some of the sermons on sex were R-rated, and we gave warnings to parents and sometimes saw whole visiting youth groups walk out blushing halfway through the sermon. On other occasions, people walked out during the sermon and flipped me off on their way out, a trend that has continued.

To survive, we had to make some big adjustments. We reached the point where we could not grow by another person, the fire department was going to shut us down, we had six services on Sundays in two locations, I had vertigo, and some people were so upset that they were showing up at my house to cuss me out face-to-face. Additionally, the people in the church were coming to services of 150 to 250 people and had the perception that they were coming to a happening small church. Consequently, they wanted the same kind of access to me and my family that they would get in a small church. The only problem was that with six services, we were not a small church but were giving the appearance that we were, which made things very difficult.

So we split the church three ways, and I functioned in an apostolic role for the three congregations that together made up Mars Hill. Mike took some of the people to start a new service in the south end of the city. Lief came on staff to run the concerts and church services at the Paradox, I took the four Ballard services, and all together we had three preachers running seven services for over one thousand people in three parts of the city, functioning as one church with one elder board and one central office. About eight hundred of the people stayed with me in the four Ballard services.

We had to quickly reorganize all of our systems and staff. Our administrative pastor, Eric, left, which we all recognized was God's call on him. And our worship leader was a great guy and great musician but was unable to coordinate the multiple bands in the three locations, so we let him go. This was one of the hardest decisions I've ever made because he was a very godly man who had worked very hard and would have been fine if the church had not gotten so crazy so quickly, and he and his very sweet wife were both close personal friends of mine. But I needed a worship pastor who could lead multiple bands, coordinate multiple services in multiple locations, and train multiple worship pastors while keeping up with a church that was growing so fast that we had no idea exactly where it was going. I had no one who could possibly fill this role but felt compelled to wait until God let me know, so I just left a gaping hole in our leadership to create a crisis that would force a leader to emerge.

A very wise friend who is a successful business entrepreneur, Jon Phelps, shared an insight with me around this time that was very clarifying. He said that in any growing organization, there are three kinds of people, and only two of them have any long-term future with a growing organization. First, there are people on the rise who demonstrate an uncanny ability to grow with the organization and become vital leaders. Second, there are people who attach themselves to the people on the rise as valuable assistants who rise by being attached to someone on the rise. Third, there are people who neither rise nor attach to anyone who is rising, and they cannot keep up with the growing demands of the organization. These people fall behind, and the organization can either allow their inability to slow down the whole team or release them and move forward without them. This is difficult to do because they are often good people who have been partly responsible for the success of the organization. But the needs of the organizational mission, not an individual in the organization, must continually remain the priority if there is to be continued success.

Up until this point, nearly everyone in the church had been connected to me, and I could no longer pull them all up with me. Simply, leaders needed to rise on their own or attach themselves to other people on the rise, or they would have to be let go.

So we made all these difficult decisions, and the church stabilized. Finally, we had facilities, money, men rising up to lead, intentional community housing, a successful concert venue, and a church that seemed organized to us. We had grown a church of one thousand people in a tough urban culture despite massive hardship. With things going so well, I feared we'd get too comfortable, and so I decided it was time to blow it all up, create some strategic chaos, and start over yet again.

Reformission Reflections

1. Which of the four elements in corporate worship is your church or ministry strongest and weakest on: singing, preaching, communion, or prayer?

2. What is the biggest hardship your church or ministry has ever faced? What is the biggest hardship your church or ministry is currently facing?

3. How have Satan and demons sought to destroy your church or ministry and your own personal life?

4. What is the biggest blessing God has ever given your church or ministry?

5. What is the biggest blessing God has ever given you personally?

6. What sinful temptation have you said no or yes to that most changed your life?

7. How well is your church or ministry doing at attracting, retaining, rebuking, inspiring, and raising up young men to be godly and masculine? What more can be done to achieve this goal?

CHAPTER SIX

I had never played in a band
or written a song when
I came to the church.

Today I am the
worship pastor.

Jesus, Today We Voted to Take a Jackhammer to Your Big Church

1,000 – 4,000 People

It was a warm spring day and I sat in my office at the church, gazing out the window at large white clouds blowing through a clear blue sky, enjoying our success. I had lost about forty pounds by shifting from the Fatkins to the Atkins diet, had paid off all the personal debts I had accrued as a broke pastor, had fixed up the old home for my family, was getting closer to my lovely wife, was enjoying my three children while looking forward to a fourth, finally owned a vehicle with less than 200,000 miles on it, and was the pastor of one of the largest churches in our city at the age of thirty-one. My eye no longer twitched, I wasn't throwing up from acid reflux, and my vertigo had cleared up.

I was sitting at my new desk, which was the first piece of furniture I had ever owned that was not a donated hand-me-down. I was sitting on a nice office chair, which someone anonymously left for me with the note "For my pastor." We owned our church building outright and had money in the bank. I had a large staff for a church our size and was sleeping like a Calvinist at nights because things were under control.

On that day I had only a few appointments, with lengthy breaks in between. I decided to walk down to the deli a few blocks away and get a Reuben sandwich on sourdough bread and some fresh air. On the way back, I walked barefoot and remember thinking that these simple pleasures had made the day one of the most relaxing and satisfying days I ever had. But by the time I walked back to the church, I realized that I was already getting bored. There was no dragon to slay, no hill to charge, no battle to fight, and no foe to conquer.

It was the winter of 2002, and our church had fought through hell and had gone from homeless to one thousand people — a big deal in Seattle. I had nearly killed myself and had gotten the church to the comfort zone.[1]

As I sat at my desk eating my sandwich, I ruminated on a simple talk that Richard DeVos, the founder of Amway, gave at our national Acts 29 conference, in which he explained four simple phases of organizational decline.[2] In what follows, I have expanded on his teaching and have reoriented it for church ministry.

Phase 1 — Creative, the dream stage
Phase 2 — Management, the reality stage
Phase 3 — Defensive justification, the failure stage
Phase 4 — Blaming, the death stage

COACHING CORNER

The comfort zone is the place a church commonly falls into once they have learned how to survive. This is the state of most American churches, with between 60 and 80 percent of all churches in America either plateaued or declining in membership and/or attendance.[3] In the comfort zone, often there is no longer a visible immediate crisis since the bills are paid, most of the big jobs are being done by someone, leaders are officially in place, a permanent facility has been secured, and the people in the church have generally grown to know and love one another. At this stage, the propensity is for the church to settle in, accept its size, and slip into a mode of maintenance. At some point, people will move away or die, others will get bored, and slowly the church will begin a cycle of decline unless it intentionally reinvents itself missionally to continue to grow by taking risks in an effort to reach lost people for Jesus.

Phase 1—Creative, the dream stage. The creative phase is the beginning of a new church or a new project within a church. This phase is marked by enthusiasm, hope, and numerous ideas that are considered for implementation, which causes momentum. The early days of our church plant were filled with this kind of creative energy, and the young and motivated people in our church were filled with ideas for all that we could do. Once we lost our building, we were thrust into another creative phase as we struggled to survive. And we returned to a creative phase when we acquired the two buildings and were able to again dream of ways to grow our ministry. I noticed that each time we were in a creative phase, our church attracted more entrepreneurial types of skilled leaders who were excited about the opportunity to try something new and make a difference in our city. This indicates that chaos and crisis can be leveraged to a church's benefit.

Phase 2—Management, the reality stage. In the management phase, the ministry project becomes a reality and requires a great deal of organization, management, and problem solving to make it successful. This phase can be a lot of hard work and is not as enthusiastically pursued because it is tedious and difficult. But without managing the creative ideas, success is not possible. We spent a few years working through very difficult management issues, such as obtaining and renovating facilities, opening a concert venue, maintaining ministry homes, and starting new services. Each of these ministries succeeded, which required increasing management, such as funding, facilities, systems, leaders, theology, and technology. The hope for every church is that they work through their management issues, thereby enabling them to return to the creative phase, where they dream up a new project and enthusiastically undertake it and raise a whole new set of management issues to overcome. Therefore, the goal of the management phase is not to get the church organized or under control. Rather, the management phase is needed to eliminate the inefficiencies and barriers that are keeping the church from refocusing back on the creative phase and creating a whole new set of problems to manage.

Phase 3 — Defensive justification, the failure stage. In the defensive justification phase, something has gone terribly wrong and has failed at the management stage. Or the church succeeded at the management stage but never returned to the creative phase and got stuck with a bunch of well-organized managers running the church but no creative and visionary new ideas to move the church forward. When this phase sets in, the church begins to stall, plateau, and slowly decline. People are less motivated to serve, money is less generously given, and a cloud of lethargy and complaint begins to settle in. This is because some leaders in the church start to act defensively and justify their failures rather than finding creative or management ways to overcome them. In this phase, time, money, and energy are spent to explain problems rather than to fix them, which is the primary clue that organizational death is on the horizon unless changes are made. Because the church is in a defensive posture, people start to leave the church, and the best and brightest people are no longer attracted to the church because it has lost sight of any risky mission that calls people to rise up in faith. The peculiar truth of the defensive justification phase is that many of the excuses provided in this season are in fact valid. But whether or not they are valid, the fact remains that they need to be overcome.

Phase 4 — Blaming, the death stage. An organization that remains stuck in the defensive justification phase for too long inevitably then declines to the blaming phase. In the blaming phase, it is obvious that the church or ministry is going to die, and excuses and explanations for the death have been devised. This does not necessarily mean that the church will be closing its doors; effectively dead churches have been known to keep the doors open on Sundays for many years to welcome a handful of people who have no mission. In this phase, the focus of the church is determining who will be blamed for the failure so that another group of people can escape responsibility for the failure. Some churches blame the pastor and fire him, others blame Satan and spiritualize everything, and still others blame the outside culture as being too dark for a church to thrive. Rarely does the leadership of a church in this phase rise up to repent of the things that are preventing the church from returning to the life-giving creative phase, and eventually the church dies. It was precisely this kind of church that gave us the free building after they died.

And it was in that building where I now sat, ruminating on all of this while eating my Reuben sandwich and gazing out the window. By the time I had finished the last bite of the adjoining pickle, I decided to start going to the mountains at least a few hours each week for silence, solitude, and prayer to ask Jesus what creative phase he wanted us to pursue next.

After a lot of long drives and walks with Jesus, I was convicted by the Holy Spirit that we had settled our management issues but needed to get back to creativity and mission because otherwise our success would become our problem. Through prayer, I came to see that we would lose our edge and settle in as yet another well-managed predictable church for a season and then decline into defensive justification and eventual death and blaming unless the elders and I as the leaders of the church returned to the creative phase and accepted that being missional involves continual risk and faith.

I feared that deconstructing and essentially restarting the church would kill us. I had found it a bit easier to take a risky gamble when we had nothing, but now we had something to lose. In the end, I realized that every person, every dollar, and every other resource belonged to Jesus and that he did not give us those treasures to bury them.

What comforted me most as I was prayerfully thinking through our next season was a lengthy study through the New Testament in which I searched for what God promises to do for the church. As I studied, I learned that God promises to grow his church, select elders, save people, bless the teaching of his Word, gift people with exactly the abilities the church needs, and providentially make up for human mistakes if people are repentant of their sins. By the end of my studies, I was confident that our future would be fine because the heavy lifting would continue to be done by Jesus and that we just needed to trust him with obedience and keep going.

At this time, I learned the difference between various types of leaders from Bob Biehl, a consultant who spoke at a small training event hosted by Leadership Network.

I could not lead the church to the next level by myself. I needed another opportunity seeker and another goal setter on my elder team to help instigate the strategic chaos of yet another creative phase. So I chose two of our best emerging leaders to prepare them for eldership to lead the next season of our church.

Jamie came to Seattle at the age of nineteen, drinking, smoking pot, and having spent most of his life driving around in a maturity cul de sac, listening to Bon Jovi albums in the great nation of Montana. In Seattle, he lived with his sister and brother-in-law, Jen and Phil, who had been with the church from the beginning. They were the first couple who showed up with kids when we were in our core phase.

Through their influence, Jamie came to faith, was baptized by me, later ran the White Horse Inn men's house, and interned under our administrative pastor, Eric, who groomed Jamie to replace him. Jamie was not formally educated and was a newer Christian but was also an incredibly gifted leader. After his one-year unpaid

COACHING CORNER

Three Types of Leaders:
1. Opportunity Seekers — continually seek new opportunities and are highly motivated by change and growth.
2. Goal Setters — make plans and break projects into phases to ensure chaos is managed so that success is achieved.
3. Problem Solvers — continually seek to understand potential problems and needs so that barriers to success can be proactively identified and removed.

internship, we hired Jamie full-time to run the church as a deacon, with the intention of growing him up to be an elder. Jamie and I got along well, and I incrementally handed more and more of the management of the church over to him. Jamie fired some of the staff and began reorganizing every aspect of the church. His decisions were very controversial, and my phone was ringing with a few angry people threatening to leave if I did not reign him in. But to override Jamie's first controversial decisions would have rendered him impotent from that point forward. I chose to support Jamie for better or worse and just accept that some people would leave the church. Whether or not he made the right choices, I knew he would learn from them and would become a phenomenal executive pastor one day. I too had made many mistakes and was given the freedom to grow into my role, and Jamie deserved the same opportunity. Over time, it became clear that Jamie was in fact right in his early controversial decisions.

I first met Tim while teaching at a conference in New Mexico for Leadership Network. He had been raised in a Baptist home in Portland and was working as a youth worship leader at a Lutheran church in Missouri. Tim and his wife, Beth, moved to Seattle simply hoping that Tim would become a guitar player in one of our worship teams. Tim and his wife lived with Grace and me for a few months until they got settled, and I saw in Tim some very strong leadership qualities that had not been cultivated. So I spent a lot of time investing in Tim, as I was with Jamie. Tim had never played in a band, written a song, or played an electric guitar. Additionally, he did not know how to sing, and it sounded like he had been hit by a car when he tried to hit high notes.

But I really liked Tim because he is one of the few manly men whom I have ever seen leading worship. I am not supposed to say this, but most of the worship dudes I have heard are not very dudely. They seem to be very in touch with their feelings and exceedingly chickified from playing too much acoustic guitar and singing prom songs to Jesus while channeling Michael Bolton and flipping their hair. Tim was a guy who brewed his own beer, smoked a pipe, rock climbed, mountain biked, river rafted, carried a knife on his belt, and talked about what he thought more than what he felt.

We clicked because I drive a 1978 Chevy truck that gets single digits to the gallon and has a bacon air freshener and no functioning speedometer and because I fashion myself as the self-appointed leader of a heterosexual male backlash in our overly chickified city filled with guys drinking herbal tea and rocking out to Mariah Carey in their lemon yellow Volkswagen Cabriolets while wearing fuchsia sweater vests that perfectly match their open-toed shoes. Anyways, Tim learned quickly, took vocal lessons, and soon assumed leadership over the entire worship department. Like Jamie, he started by firing most everyone and started over from scratch.

As opportunity seeking leaders well-suited for the creative phase, Jamie, Tim, and I began envisioning what the next phase of the church should look like if we hoped to stay on mission. I decided to never view our church as a church but rather always to view it like a church planter with a core group launching out to reach the city. Now we simply had a core of one thousand instead of the original twelve that began in the living room of my home.

I started studying the major differences between smaller and larger churches. My hope was to first understand the dynamics of a large church and then plan with the elders to build that larger church. As I studied, a few dozen items particularly struck me, and I gleaned other insights from observing larger churches.[4]

I began writing out how I envisioned our church at 3,000-plus people. I chose this number because roughly half of all megachurches have between 2,000 and 3,000 people, and the other half have over 3,000 people, according to a conversation with John Vaughan of Church Growth Today. This means that the 3,000 barrier is the most difficult of any church size to overcome. Therefore, it seemed prudent to push for that goal with plans to reorganize if and when we got over the 3,000 mark.

So I began to reverse-engineer a plan for our church to grow to more than three thousand people with help from Jamie and Tim. In the end, we decided that what was in the best interests of our mission to the city was not in the best interests of each of our elders. I knew God was compelling me to state the vision to the elders. And I knew that the vision would quite possibly split the church three ways between the founders—Lief, Mike, and me. Nonetheless, I met with our elders to seek their input on the recommended changes, knowing it could undo all that we had worked so hard to accomplish. We spent a lengthy day going over the proposal, and things were tense.

Mike and two elders chose to take their church service out as a separate church plant. This decision was tough because I genuinely loved Mike, and still do. He was an older man who had faithfully encouraged and supported me through the toughest times in our church. But he wanted his own pulpit and felt called to a mission in a different part of the city and would need to be released so that we could each follow the mission Jesus had called us to. Many of our people loved Mike and would leave with him, which meant we might take a hit in terms of leaders and dollars. But it was the right thing to do for the gospel.

I asked my dear friend and accountability partner, Lief, to shut down the Paradox because the concerts were losing a lot of money, give up the pulpit, and become the associate pastor. Lief tearfully agreed to shoot his dream and do what was best for the whole church.

In shutting down the Paradox, we also had to let go of two very godly young deacons named Jeff and Josh. Josh had lived at my house and demonstrated gifts in both teaching and leadership but was just not yet ready to run that ministry by himself. Jeff was and is a well-known punk musician in our area who has fronted bands like 90 Pound Wuss and Suffering and the Hideous Thieves. The Paradox kids loved Jeff, and when they found out that we were shutting the concert venue down and releasing Jeff, many of them were very angry because to them everyone at the Paradox was a family and we had ruined it. Our credibility with the music scene largely came down to how Jeff would respond. If he got bitter, we were doomed and would get smeared in the local alternative press, have at least a hundred young punk-rock fans leave our church, and see yet another collapse in our worship department as the many musicians who loved Jeff departed.

To Jeff's credit, he was the biggest defender of the church during this difficult season and lovingly led the young indie and punk-rock fans to stick with the church and trust the elders. Today Jeff remains a vital church member, helping to lead worship as the bass player in Team Strikeforce. God has honored him with a great job in the entertainment industry, a beautiful wife, and two of the most adorable children God has ever given one of his sons. I will forever remain grateful to Jeff for his sacrifice to our mission. He is one of the great unsung heroes in the history of our church because he did what was best for the church instead of what was best for him, and God blessed both him and our church for it.

I asked the elders to shut down the Noonday women's home despite the fact that it had led many women to Jesus and had done much good for our church. Simply, it was losing money and was some $20,000 in debt.

I also asked the elders to shut down the White Horse Inn men's home despite the fact that leaders such as Jamie were raised up from within the house. Like nearly all of our staff members over the years, these young leaders worked full-time for a year as unpaid interns before coming on as paid staff because we could not initially afford to pay them. But a lesser quality of men had moved into the house, and they were not very ministry-minded. Instead, we were focusing our energies on encouraging solid married couples to purchase larger homes that could accommodate renters and guests to provide community living opportunities without the financial burden being placed upon the church.

I asked the elders to centralize all of Mars Hill into our small church building and run four services there. We needed to cut our costs, cut our staff, and raise money to purchase a much larger building that would seat at least a thousand people, which would radically change our entire church and likely cause some people to leave.

Through reading books[5] and speaking with pastors of large churches — such as Wayne Cordero, Michael Slaughter, Tim Keller, Larry Osborne, Leith Anderson, Robert Lewis, and Rick Warren — in conversations that lasted from a few minutes to a few hours, I started to better understand how we would need to change if the church were to be able to continue to innovate and grow. Ten principles in particular stuck with me.

1. I needed to transition from caring for all the people to ensuring they were all cared for by raising up elders, deacons, and church members.

2. I needed to transition from being everyone's pastor to being the missiologist-preacher who led the church from the Bible in the pulpit.

3. I needed to stop doing most of the work I was doing and deploy more elders and deacons to manage church members who would do the work of the ministry.

4. I needed to transition from working both in the church and on the church to almost exclusively working on the church, continually making plans to connect the Bible with our culture, like Paul did as a missiologist-apostle.

5. Our internal and external church communication needed to transition from informal and oral to written and formal, which would include me writing lots of email templates, booklets, and position papers to inform our people.

6. We needed to transition our people from a survivalist mentality that focused on the present to a settler mentality that focused on a lasting legacy.

7. We needed our people to accept that we would be a very large church.

8. We needed to ensure that in the tension between caring for Christians and reaching non-Christians, evangelism continually remained our highest priority.

9. We needed to accept the fact that some people would feel less connected to my family and me, experience displacement, and leave the church.

10. My wife and I needed to reserve the right to select our own friends without feeling personally obligated to everyone in the church.

To make these transitions, I needed to hand much of my workload to my elders and deacons so that I could continue to concentrate on the future expansion of our church. In some ways, I longed for this day because it meant the weight of the church would be off of my shoulders and shared with many leaders. In other ways, I lamented not being able to invest in every young couple, experience the joy of officiating at so many weddings, or know everything that was going on in the church.

I asked our newest and oldest elder, Bent, to take over the counseling load that I had been carrying. He was the first person to join our church who had gray hair, and he and his cute Filipino wife, Joanne, were like rock stars with groupies since all the young people wanted to hang out with these grandparents that loved Jesus. My problem was I loved our people so much that if I got deeply involved in the pain of too many people's lives, it emotionally killed me, and I needed to do less counseling.

I asked Lief to take over all of the premarital counseling and weddings for me. I asked Jamie to manage the staff, the budget, and all the hiring and firing. I also met with one of our newer elders, and we decided that he should transition to a church we had helped plant in the suburbs, because it was a better fit for him than where we were going. By this point, Lief and I were the only founding elders who remained at the church.

I simply stopped being the hub in the church around which everything else revolved. I focused on reaching the city, raising money, acquiring a building, leading the church, assisting church planters, and training more leaders. I changed my email address so that I could not be easily found and also changed my home phone and cell phone numbers. I also informed my wife that we would move to a new home because everyone knew where we lived and I needed to be less accessible.

The elders unanimously approved the entire master plan, though it cost almost every one of them personal power and gave them much more work. The elders remained unified through this season of enormous change as we took a jackhammer to the church we had worked so hard to build.

Knowing that our church members would feel displaced and would still need a way to connect, deacon Jason and a church member named Mark put together a password-protected website exclusively for church members, with discussion threads, classifieds, prayer requests, and a directory. It soon became the buzzing hub of our growing church.

One Sunday shortly after the elders had given their approval, I notified the church of the plan. Despite the fact that we were losing Mike and three other elders as well as some deacons and key families, shutting down two ministry homes, canceling a concert venue, and transitioning from a church with seven Sunday services in three locations to one church with four services in one location, not one member scheduled a meeting with an elder to question what we were proposing, and no one resigned membership during the entire restart. Our members were clearly with us on the mission and trusted their elders to lead them, which was very comforting and reassuring.

We purchased a twenty-year-old, 40,000-square-foot former hardware store Jamie had found in an industrial area two miles from the old church that had been given to us. It was in a hip part of the city, a short walk from the studio where Nirvana and other bands recorded their albums. The purchase price was about $3.7 million, and we needed to raise about $1 million for the construction costs of getting it up to code. We pulled some of the equity out of our small building. Our people put in thousands of hours of donated labor and gave all the money they could. But we were still $120,000 short as we approached the end of the project, and we desperately needed the money.

The elders had vowed not to hire a fundraising consultant or do anything gimmicky to raise the money. So we called a rare church meeting in the warehouse space, which had been gutted and was filled with dust and unfinished projects. Tim played his guitar and we all sang songs of worship. Jamie, Lief, and I each spoke to the church, telling them our vision for the space and how much money we needed. Jamie was to close the meeting in prayer. We did not intend to take an offering that night. But as Jamie went up to pray, someone pulled him aside and informed him that they would match every dollar that people gave or pledged that night, up to $60,000. Stunned, Jamie stood up and informed everyone.

The three hundred or so young and broke people present were shocked. A buzz hit the room as people started talking, praying, praising God, and emptying their pockets. We grabbed some buckets, and people gave their cash, wrote checks, and gave pledges. It felt like one of those God moments in Acts, and our people were filled with awe as God showed up in our midst. A lot of people left in tears that night, and we rushed up to our offices to count the offering. It totaled $60,000. With the matching pledge, it was exactly what we needed.

We entered our new building in March of 2003 with about 1,600 people in attendance. Our first Sunday service in the new building opened in prayer to God, thanking him for the new building and asking him to allow us to outgrow it as quickly as possible. As I had done for the first launch of the church, I preached through Ecclesiastes, though I did a much better job this time because I connected every sermon to Jesus. We soon settled in at about 1,200 people a week between the two services (10:00 a.m. and 5:00 p.m.), in a room that seated about 1,300 people.

When we opened the new facility, we couldn't afford chairs, so people brought their own, and we had an assortment of lawn chairs, folding chairs, deck chairs, and dining chairs. Within a few months, someone who remains anonymous to this day came one Sunday and wrote a $20,000 check for new chairs. I think it was an angel.

Our sound system was woefully inadequate for the new space, and on opening day of the new building, an entertainment mogul grabbed Tim and me and pledged a new sound system. He also provided a wonderful Christian brother named Bill Platt, who had been one of the chief sound designers for Disney, as our designer. We were then given perhaps $500,000 worth of sound gear by one kind and generous family.

Tim became the worship pastor and built an enormous department with multiple bands, lighting engineers, sound engineers, and video camera operators. We even got a choir for holidays and a baptismal in which to dunk the new converts on Sundays.

Shortly thereafter, we caught a media buzz that included a twelve-page feature on us in the *Seattle Times*, which led to me becoming one of their new religion columnists.[6] Since then, we have received a lot of great press from local magazines, television stations, and radio stations. The most curious article was in *Seattle* magazine, which named me one of the twenty-five most powerful people in Seattle, a big honor.[7] Over the years, we have found that by making friendly relationships with various media gatekeepers and sending out press releases for story and photo opportunities, we have received an overwhelming amount of positive local media coverage in every medium from television to radio, magazines, and newspapers, including some of the most extreme alternative-lifestyle and militant liberal publications.

We continually upgraded our Gospel Class membership process, which grew to be as large as four hundred people a quarter. At the end of the class, people may become members after an interview to ensure they are saved, answer any final questions, and determine where to plug them in for learning and service. About half of the people who take the class decide not to become members and often leave the church because they disagree with our doctrines or with aspects of our mission that we are simply unwilling to negotiate on.

Our membership has always equaled about one-third of our Sunday attendance, since Sunday attendance includes non-Christians, people who are getting to know us well enough to decide if they want to become members, and curious people just checking us out. We also have a large number of pastors from other churches attending our evening services just for refreshment, which we welcome as a way to serve them.

Our ecclesiology seems to be working. Our present weekly attendance has climbed from 1,200 to over 4,000 people in just two years, and we have only six paid elders-pastors on staff, though that number will be increasing. Though only in his midtwenties, Jamie has become the executive pastor, has done a fabulous job running the church, was elected as the president of the local chamber of commerce by the business community, and was named one of the top church administrators in the country.

Lief's premarital class now prepares over one hundred couples for marriage each year. Helping coordinate the weddings are ten volunteer deacons led by a wonderful woman named Judy, who came to Christ during the premarital class Grace and I hosted in our home in the early days of the church.

Many of our couples are having fairly large families, which is unusual in Seattle, which has less children than any U.S. city other than San Francisco and more dogs than children.[8] Our church is averaging a few births every week, and our children's ministry has exploded under the leadership of a great married couple, Dick, who is a pastor, and Tami, who is a deacon. Dick writes curriculum for the kids, and our artists create the coloring sheets for the smaller kids, all based on the same text that I am preaching from each week so that families are studying a book of the Bible together. We still transition children into the main service as early as possible, ideally before age ten.

We keep sending out church planters and use over 10 percent of our general tithes and offerings to support church planters. Some of our best and longest-term people go out with the new plants because they have caught the missional bug. Steve Tompkins has come on as a paid elder to oversee our church-planting ministry as the director of the Acts 29 Network.[9] Steve is in his forties and is a former church planter and senior pastor with two Master's degrees in theology. He had left formal ministry and was a faithful member of our church with his wise wife and two great kids before we hired him. The first time I met Steve, he and his son Sam were picking up trash after one of the church services, which indicates Steve's humility and love for our church.

We have added a number of new elders. One of them is a very bright young man in his twenties named Mike, who moved from Joplin, Missouri, to Seattle to work at Microsoft. I have taught at conferences in Joplin a few times and must report that it is among the most peculiar places on earth. First, every item on every menu at every restaurant comes covered in gravy. Second, the town is filled with large fireworks stands because rednecks apparently like things that blow up. Third, the big employer in town is FAG ball bearings, and the town is filled with large white billboards that simply say FAG in large black letters (I am not making this up). Anyway, Mike has taken over our exploding small group ministry to finally organize it and give it sorely needed leadership. He is well-suited for the position because it is growing and complicated and he is a problem-solving type of leader. Along with Mike, two new elders have risen up to help build a sufficient number of home-based small groups. Brad is a young engineer, and Dave is a longtime Navigators staff member in his midsixties.

One of our young elders in his twenties, Gary, has started a free Bible Institute called Capstone to better train our church members. Gary started attending the church when he was a student and football player at the University of Washington. He was trained by Mike Gunn and went on to finish his Master's degree in theology. Some people have been frustrated because we only allow members to take classes, but we have simply held the line that we do not want consumers receiving training from our leaders. We want to make sure that people are Christians and are committed to our mission before we are willing to invest in them to any significant degree.

Pastor Bent has launched a number of care and recovery groups for such things as sexual abuse, sexual addiction, and alcoholism. He is also training new elders to help shoulder this burden with him. Among them is Phil, who was the first father to show up at our church when we had less than forty people and who has risen up to become a pastor.

Now that we have our own building, we are also able to host conferences and large concerts. The highlight of these events was a theology conference with Dr. John Piper speaking.[10]

Our elders, deacons, and church members are generally doing a phenomenal job. If we were a typical consumer-based church that pays people to minister to the congregation instead of a missional church that pays leaders to equip the congregation to do ministry, we would have to hire at least one hundred full-time people to make up for the hours our people volunteer. For example, some weekends we have as many as five thousand people come through the building for various events. Amazingly, we do not have a paid janitor, and the entire building is maintained by an army of volunteers.

Our musical style has broadened to include indie rock, rockabilly, folk, and old-school country and blues under Tim's leadership.[11] The worship experience in our big room has changed greatly, from being a horizontal experience in which you know the people leading worship from the stage and those singing around you to being a vertical experience, in which the focus is more on personally connecting with God. Now that we also have video cameras, we often baptize new converts and dedicate children, to keep the values of new birth and birth before our people. The Sunday production has gotten complicated enough to require a few hundred volunteers at each of our four current services (double the number we had upon entering the building two years prior) to pull everything off and a paid full-time event deacon, Jeff, to manage the mayhem.

Pastor James continues to lead our monthly film and theology class, at which attendance rises to more than two hundred people depending on the film. He continues to show an occasional unedited R-rated movie to train our people to think critically about the themes preached through film, which is the new cultural form of preaching. James also shows a G-rated family-friendly film periodically to train children to critically interpret what they watch so that they too can be good missionaries in our culture.

Our outdoor ministry, which began in 1999 with Pastor Mike before he went out to plant his own church, continues to host events such as rock climbing, kayaking, snowshoeing, and other sports. Today, unpaid church members run these events.

The Paradox was shut down for over a year until we got enough money to remodel a warehouse portion of our new building as the new Paradox. The new room is nicer and the sound equipment is better than at the old venue. A businessman who does not attend our church read about us in the *Seattle Times*, and after meeting with me, he agreed to give us $5,000 a month for the first few months of concerts at the new Paradox. This enabled Bubba, who was a deacon and is now an elder, and his army of indie-rock volunteers, many of whom are not yet Christians, to run a lot of free concerts and draw the young fan base back to the shows. We also have the big room, which has housed some very large concerts for more than 1,800 people. We also host a non-Christian jazz festival that boasts some world-renowned musicians along with free clinics for young student musicians, thereby providing us with a great opportunity to practice hospitality to our city.

We also had to cancel our weekly summer outdoor Bible study, which had been running since we were a handful of people, in favor of multiple studies scattered in various parks around the region. It had grown too large to fit in any of the city parks that would welcome us. In our final year of the weekly all-church summer study, we had baptisms in Lake Union, which over-looks the city, and the *Seattle Times* came out and took photo-graphs. On the front page of the paper was an enormous photo of us baptizing new converts with a backdrop of the skyline of one of America's least churched cities. But when we went to con-duct more baptisms a few weeks later in the same location, the harbor police showed up in their patrol boat, threatened to cite us for being in city water, and made a mess of our baptism by yelling at us through their bullhorn. We just ignored them and kept baptizing the new converts. To be honest, it ticked me off. In the same area where we were baptizing people, an annual solstice parade is held for eco-whacko earth worshipers, complete with a nudist bicycling team that no one complains about— and we were getting yelled at by cops with bullhorns for conducting baptisms.

In addition to the many changes we have made, we have had to repent of our idealism on two matters and start ministries we swore we never would. When we started the church, I emphatically said that we would only have age-integrated ministries because various life stages and generations are supposed to love each other as the church, not be isolated from each other in departments of the church. As a general rule, I still believe this and we still practice it. But we now have a ministry for singles. And I am the primary teacher in the high school ministry, which I repeatedly vowed we would never have.

We still do not offer adult Sunday school classes, for four reasons. First, such classes discourage people from bringing lost friends to church because their friends likely would not want to attend both a church service and a more intimate class generally suited for Christians. Second, we believe community group Bible studies in homes better suit our values of scattering around the region in the less formal setting of a home, where multiple life stages and generations can more easily coexist and lost neighbors can be reached for Jesus. Third, we do not have enough classroom space or parking to simultaneously accommodate church services and Sunday school classes, and the high cost of real estate in our city makes it unlikely that we ever will. Fourth, we want our evening classes to run for only a quarter so that people can get formal teaching in classes as needed but have ongoing relationships with people in community groups.

My role has also changed greatly. I make more time to study and write and work from my home library. This is a tremendous help. For the first time, I am able to separate my office at the church, where I meet with people, and my study at home, where I research and write. I now split the week between three days at the church for meetings and services and three days working from home, with one day off. Over the years, I have discovered that a pastor needs both an office set up like a living room at the church for meetings and a library at home for studying without constant interruption. I also hired a male executive assistant, like Joseph, to work closely with me, in an effort to not be yet another pastor with a sick story about getting entangled with his assistant.

The many changes in my role came about through some life-changing conversations. Just before we passed the three-thousand mark, I met with a number of pastors who lead very large churches, whom I met through Leadership Network, to glean insights from them. No book has been written for churches of our size because there are only about 425 churches in that range, according to a conversation I had with megachurch expert John Vaughan of Church Growth Today, therefore no market exists for such a book.

Every pastor I met with mentioned one fact that was particularly troubling. At each transition from one size barrier to another, one of two things happens to a church. One, the lead pastor reorganizes the church and hands off more power and control to other leaders, which means that some people are let go, while others are reassigned or given less power than they were hoping for. Consequently, those people who are not kept at the center of power become disgruntled, band together, and attempt to lead a coup, which undermines the lead pastor. Two, the lead pastor senses the resistance to change from his leaders and chooses not to make the difficult decisions regarding reorganization and instead continues to do too much, which leads to his burnout and breakdown. Indeed, growing a church is often a lose-lose scenario.

In some of the worst scenarios I have seen, pastors completely crack and have nervous breakdowns, work so many hours that their marriages and families crumble, or venture into sin, such as drugs, alcohol, and sex, for relief from the pressure.

One pastor I will not name particularly terrified me. He wanted so badly to escape the pressure of ministry that he actually weighed his options for self-destruction. He committed adultery with a female church leader to get fired, have people hate him, and be done with the church without having to deal with the pain of people trying to bring him back.

These sort of frank insights were terrifying and sobering. Over the years, Grace and I had made great strides in our marriage, and I had finally gotten my life in order so that I was generally healthy physically, spiritually, mentally, emotionally, and financially. As Mars Hill rocketed toward the four-thousand mark, I feared what might happen to my children and my wife if the horror stories I heard from the other pastors ahead of me became reality. So I shifted my energies to developing other leaders, particularly fellow elders, who would work in the church so that I could work on the church and plan for our future growth. The details of what we learned and how we planned for healthy growth are the subject of the next chapter.

Reformission Reflections

1. Is your church or ministry currently in the creative, management, defensive justification, or blaming stage? Why do you think so?

2. On a scale of 1 to 10, with 1 being poor and 10 being excellent, how well has your church or ministry done at raising up people from within to lead? What should be done to improve this? Is there a clear path for leadership development for those aspiring to become leaders?

3. When is the last time your church or ministry took a big risk? How did it turn out?

4. Is there any big risk that your church or ministry should be taking in the near future?

5. Name one occasion when you saw God show up in such an amazing way that it built your faith and filled you with awe.

CHAPTER SEVEN

Jesus, We're Loading Our Squirt Guns to Charge Hell Again

4,000 – 10,000 People

In the fall of 2004, Leadership Network brought together a handful of large-church pastors for a meeting in New York. It was an honor to be among such successful and diverse pastors as Wayne Cordero (Foursquare), Tim Keller (Presbyterian), Michael Slaughter (Methodist), Walt Kallestad (Lutheran), and Matt Hannan and Bob Roberts (Baptist). Each of them had timely insights that helped clarify the plans I was making to grow our church to ten thousand people. During one of the breaks, I grabbed lunch with Larry Osborne, who pastors North Coast, a church of six thousand people in San Diego, California. Our church had quickly blown through the three-thousand mark, and we were expecting to crest at just under four thousand people a week by the fast-approaching spring of 2005.

I was in the middle of putting together a comprehensive strategic plan for the future of our church, with plans to grow to over ten thousand people. Our two morning and two evening Sunday services were all filling up, and we needed to decide what our next steps would be. We searched diligently but once again could not find a facility with three thousand seats or more to rent in the city. And we were unwilling to relocate the church out of the city, where land was cheaper and more options were available.

As I sat with Larry, I immediately launched into a barrage of questions about growing the church, hoping to maximize our time together. Larry had impressively grown his church from a small congregation to a church of six thousand people while maintaining sound doctrine and incorporating an effective small group ministry.

Larry proceeded to ignore all of my questions and instead started asking me questions seemingly unrelated to growing the church. He asked me how many children I had, their ages, the condition of my marriage, and if being a good husband and father was more important to me than growing a large church.

I was stunned. Over the years, I had met with many successful pastors to learn from them. Not one of them had ever asked anything about my personal life and my family or even if I was morally fit to be a pastor. The only people who ever asked those types of questions were my elders, because they love me and my family.

To be honest, I care very little whether I pastor a large church. I enjoy my ministry very much, especially preaching the Bible and helping young church planters chase their dreams. But far more than anything that pertains to church work, I prefer taking my oldest daughter out for breakfast each Tuesday before school, bike riding with my oldest son, taking my middle son to the pet store to see the animals, taking my youngest daughter on walks, cuddling with my baby boy, and going out on our weekly date night with my wife, who has been my love since we met at age seventeen.

I work hard and long hours but try to do as much work from home as possible. I usually have dinner with my family every night except Friday, which is my weekly date night with my wife, and Sunday, because I'm preaching the evening services.

Larry's simple questions struck at the core of who I am. I am a Christian first. Husband second. Daddy third. And pastor fourth. I enjoy ministry, but I live for Jesus and my family. My sermons are filled with comedic rants about my five kids (three boys and two girls). I have learned over the years not to shelter my kids from my work but instead to take them with me on hospital visits and such to learn to share the gospel and pray for people, because my kids are my first disciples and I enjoy them.

Larry talked openly about some hard days in his church over the years and kindly asked me to build a church that I could pastor as a healthy man with a healthy family for the rest of my life. He said that as my children got older, they would need me at their games and activities and that my energy level would diminish as I got older, thereby not allowing me to keep the frantic pace I had set for myself in my twenties.

As he spoke, I scribbled out pages of notes because the Holy Spirit was speaking through my Christian brother, who was giving me permission to do what I knew in my gut was right but felt guilty for executing because it seemed selfish. But it had also dawned on me that in many churches, everyone and everything is cared for except the lead pastor and his family, who are not protected as an important asset.

Larry warned me against creating a church that was essentially a giant monster that would devour my joy, my marriage, and my children. He explained how he was able to lead a large church while still coaching his son's sports teams without missing any games. This really hit home for me because my dad was a union drywaller who came home from backbreaking work every night to coach my baseball team in his steel-toed boots and to spend time with his three sons and two daughters. I wanted a life off the stage with my wife and kids more than I wanted a life on the stage without them.

Larry counseled me not to start the Saturday evening service that I was planning. His reasoning was that in a few years, my five young kids would all be in school during the week and I would be at church preaching all day on Sunday. This would leave only Saturday as the one day each week that our whole family could be together. If I preached a Saturday evening service, I would spend the day preparing and would give away the only day I had with my family. Additionally, since most of our church leaders were getting married and having children, they too would be sacrificing their family time, and we would end up with a large church marked by leaders with neglected marriages and children. His counsel was tremendously helpful and saved me from returning to a new cycle of unhealthy burnout, which I had spent the past years trying to escape from. Simply, he was instructing me on the chief principles for creating a mature missional church.[1]

So I tried to begin with the end in mind. I sought to plan for our church for as far down the road as I could see. I could envision a church of more than ten thousand people and began working with Jamie to reverse-engineer a plan to become that church. We drafted a strategic plan that was over a hundred pages long, between plans and supporting documents and articles. We then presented our strategic plan to the elders and deacons, who helped us make some changes that greatly improved the plan. The deacons and elders also devised strategic plans so that their areas of ministry could grow with the church. If all of the plans were put together, the total master plan would be hundreds of pages long.

Our strategic plan, which is sketched out in this chapter, won't be fully implemented until after this book is published. By that time, we will know if we had a good plan or if we messed everything up and reduced the church to a small group of people meeting in a phone booth and grumbling about the strategic plan. I am hesitant to end the book with these details because I have no guarantee that they will work. But it's where we are at, going into another season of great risk.

COACHING CORNER

Maturity is the point at which the senior leader(s) again calls the church to the mission that Jesus has called them to accomplish. As a church reaches maturity, it in some ways returns to a relaunching phase, in which the church organizes itself for growth but in a very thoughtful and wise way, seeking to maximize all their resources to achieve their goals. Mature churches are known for such things as well-developed systems, policies, procedures, communication forms (internal and external), and leadership development tracts, which make it easy for ministry to be done well. A mature church has all the zeal of an infant church but has over time also learned how to conduct itself with the kind of wisdom that makes the church most effective.

One of the hardest parts of leading Mars Hill has been the steep learning curve. This is the first church I have ever pastored or have even been an official member of. Many of my staff and elders are similarly inexperienced with a ministry of this size. We are growing so fast that systems are being outgrown before they are even built. According to John Vaughan of Church Growth Today, the typical church of four thousand generally takes many years to pass the two-thousand barrier, as the following statistics show, and we have accomplished that feat by God's grace in just eight years from a humble beginning of three couples and a few singles.[2]

One of the major difficulties in planning for our future is trying to project our rate of future growth so that we can reverse-engineer the systems to care for that many people effectively while also sending good people out to plant more churches. The trick is not to expect too much and then hit a financial crisis or to expect too little and burn out an insufficient staff. As we look down the road, the following changes are on our immediate horizon, and I am sure there are things we have missed and changes we will make to our changes depending on what happens next. Whatever happens next, we'll pray for wisdom and figure it out. In the meantime, the following items are what I am burdened for in terms of our future.

How Long it Took Churches over 4,000 People to Reach 2,000 in Attendance

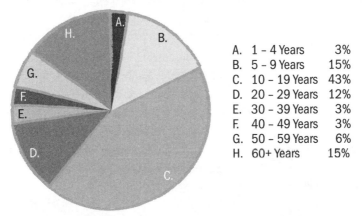

A.	1 – 4 Years	3%
B.	5 – 9 Years	15%
C.	10 – 19 Years	43%
D.	20 – 29 Years	12%
E.	30 – 39 Years	3%
F.	40 – 49 Years	3%
G.	50 – 59 Years	6%
H.	60+ Years	15%

More Prayerful Men

Functionally, my devotional life is a bit mystical, like Jonathan Edwards' was, so it would make most charismatic Christians happy even though I've never spoken in tongues. I spend a lot of time in prayer, silence, solitude, study, and the other contemplative disciplines to hear from and connect with Jesus. I do believe that God is sovereign over all of life and that the Holy Spirit will guide me through all of life if I walk in step with him. Corporately, however, I have struggled with how to more effectively implement prayer churchwide. Right now we leave time in our church service for people to pray. We have prayer requests continually posted on our church members' website. People pray for one another in their community groups. And after church, people can come forward for prayer with a church leader.

But I do not believe we are praying as strategically as we could or should be. So I am beginning an early morning prayer meeting for our men before they head to work and am using that time to keep them abreast of the most urgent needs in our city and church so that they can pray together effectively. Also, with so many men wanting to be closer to the center of the action in the church, the prayer meeting will allow men motivated to become leaders to prove their commitment by getting up early and marching forward on their knees.

More Elders

If our church is to grow, we will need far more elders to care for our people. The church is too big and there is too much going on for one team of elders to manage the church's daily operations and plan for the future. Even the simple task of officiating weddings for a church of ten thousand young people is nearly impossible unless there is an army of pastors since the projected number of weddings is equivalent to one every day of the year. The problem, however, is that when there are more than eight or ten elders, the management and unity of the elders is nearly impossible to maintain.

The New Testament is very clear on the functions of elders (leading, disciplining, teaching, shepherding, praying, etc.) and the qualifications of an elder (e.g., 1 Tim. 3:1 – 7; Titus 1:5 – 9).[3] But the New Testament is not clear on how the elders should be organized because the form must be adapted for the various cultures that have now had church elders for two thousand years. Therefore, the New Testament does not tell us how many elders a local church should have, how often they should meet, how they should conduct their vote (e.g., unanimity, consensus, majority), or how they should be organized. The New Testament assumes that qualified elders who love God's people will organize themselves according to the leading of the Holy Spirit.

So I began researching the various ways we could organize our elders, reading a great number of books and meeting with a number of pastors from larger churches. A great deal could be said about leading an elder team, and I hope to write a book on this subject, but here I will simply summarize some of the more pertinent points.

Options for Elder Organization

Elder Organization Option 1: A Closed Number of Elders
In this format, the number of elders has a set maximum, and like musical chairs, once the seats are filled, no new elders are appointed until a position opens up.

Pros	Cons
· A small and static number of elders is easier to manage. · Quick decision-making is possible.	· The elders may become overworked. · The people may suffer if membership grows and the number of elders does not. · The church is unable to grow because of a lack of leadership. · Men unable to become elders may leave to seek opportunities elsewhere, taking energy and ideas with them and leaving an aging and static leadership elder team.

Elder Organization Option 2: An Open Number of Elders
In this format, the number of elders is not limited, which allows for a very large team of elders. The elders all function as equals and vote on issues pertaining to the leadership of the church.

Pros	Cons
· The leadership may develop an unlimited number of elders. · Young men from within the church can rise up to become elders.	· Managing multiple elders is difficult. · Keeping unpaid elders up to speed on all the issues is difficult. · Decision-making is a slower process. · Arranging times when everyone can meet becomes very difficult. · Every elder is expected to be a generalist and keep up with the whole church. · Having real community between all of the men and between their families is very difficult.

Elder Organization Option 3: Rotating Terms
In this format, paid elders continually serve as elders but unpaid elders rotate on and off the team after serving set terms (e.g., two to three years).

Pros	Cons
· The leadership may develop many elders but keep a smaller board.	· Managing a large number of elders and their rotations is difficult. · Getting new elders up to speed on existing projects is difficult. · Building momentum and continuity is difficult with fixed term lengths. · Elders who do not rotate hold more power than those who do.

Elder Organization Option 4: Split Elder and Pastor Roles
In this format, a distinction is made between an elder, who is unpaid (often a skilled businessman) and a pastor, who is paid. The

unpaid elders have authority over the paid pastors, though some pastors, such as the senior pastor, could also be elders.

Pros	Cons
· Pastors don't have to deal with as many business issues and can focus on shepherding people.	· A distinction should not be made between elders and pastors (e.g., Acts 20:27 – 28; 1 Peter 5:1 – 2).
	· Authority lines become very unclear, and conflict between the elders and pastors is likely.
	· The most theological men do not have the most authority.
	· The leaders most closely connected to the people in the church do not make the final decisions for their care.

In the end, I was not impressed with any of these options for our growing church. So I proposed that we needed to have both one large elder team that made churchwide decisions and various smaller elder teams making decisions for their ministry areas in the church. There is precedence for a large team of elders. Some historians have suggested that the church in Jerusalem may have had seventy elders since that was the number of members in the Jewish Sanhedrin. It seemed obvious that if we wanted our elders to do the duties of a New Testament pastor, we would perhaps need that many elders if our church continued to grow.

But the thought of having seventy generalists voting on every detail of church business sounded like an arduously slow death by committee. So while we wanted to have as many elders as God would raise up, we also needed to find a way to manage which issues they would vote on so that things did not continually bottleneck with the elders. This led to a lot of discussion among our elders about what we would vote on as an entire team and what percentage would be required for a proposal to be approved.

Options for Elder Voting

As I studied, only two real options surfaced. Both options would be a major change from our previous way of operating. Until this point, every elder had voted on every matter. Each of our options eliminated one or the other variable so that not every elder voted or every elder voted but not on every matter. These two options are summarized below.

Elder Voting Option 1: Voting and Non-Voting Elders

In this format, we could have a very large elder board that would be present at every meeting and free to speak on the issues, but only some elders (e.g., between four and eight) would vote on church-wide matters.

Pros	Cons
· The church benefits from the input of all the elders on various issues. · The church benefits from having multiple elders. · The elder team benefits from needing fewer people to meet for a vote and to agree for action to be taken.	· A discrepancy in power is created between voting and non-voting elders, which could lead to conflict among the elders.

Elder Voting Option 2: Delineated Voting

In this scenario, all elders would vote, but only on selected issues vital to the health of the entire church. All other issues would be voted on by teams of elders overseeing their particular areas of ministry. For example, over the worship department, biblical counseling department, small groups department, administration department, church planting department, and so on, would be teams of elders who would lead and govern their ministry areas. These smaller teams of elders would meet separately from the entire elder board to vote on their area of ministry without needing to involve all of the elders. The only issues that would require a vote from all of the elders would be as follows:

- Theology—the adoption of a new doctrine or alteration of an existing doctrine.
- Property—the purchase or sale of a facility or property.
- Eldership—the approval or discipline of a fellow elder.
- Sites—the opening or closing of a new ministry site.
- Budget—the gross budget (not each line item).
- Other—any other written proposal drafted by any elder can be brought before all the elders, providing it is approved by the moderating elder.

In this scenario, all frontline ministry decisions would be made by the smaller elder teams and would not come before all of the elders unless proposed and approved by the moderating elder, who functions as the gatekeeper to prevent elders from dropping issues into the meetings without prior approval. Smaller working teams of elders would also be brought together for specific projects according to their spiritual gifts and experience. These teams would generate proposals, which would then be considered by all the elders. Examples of such projects would include:

- staff salaries
- hiring and firing of paid deacons and other paid staff
- annual elder performance reviews
- budget line items
- real estate acquisitions

As we considered this seemingly innovative way of organizing our elders, the benefits and risks became evident.

In the end, our elders voted to not limit the size of the elder team or impose term limits for elders and adopted Elder Voting Option 2 to maintain order and efficiency. This decision could easily have split the elder team. Thankfully, a great deal of prayer and thoughtful discussion among the elders preceded these decisions and was very helpful in increasing our unity and loving trust. This experience was incredibly encouraging to me because each elder laid down his interests to do what was best for the whole church

Pros	Cons
· The church can have a large number of elders. · The departmental elder teams can make decisions quickly. · Each elder has a realm of great authority and responsibility. · The most informed people can make decisions without having to catch other elders up to speed.	· If the elders are not unified and communicating, the departmental elder teams could turn into divisive factions. · If the lead pastor does not provide clear, unifying leadership, the overall elder team could fragment.

because he believed it was the will of Jesus, our Senior Pastor. My pastoral duties now reside mainly in caring for a church of over seventy people—the elders and their wives and children.

More Technology

Our main website has successfully become our new front door, and our members' website has become our new living room. Currently, our main website is version 3.5 and is on pace for over one million annual MP3 downloads of free sermons and live recordings of our worship bands. Our password-protected members' website has over 1,200 users and over 30,000 postings on over 4,000 topics.

To serve our growing church in Microsoftville, we need to increase not only the physical capacity of our church but the digital capacity as well. Our software worked well when our church was smaller but is now incapable of keeping up, particularly as we prepare to transition to multiple locations and to have pastors working remotely from home.

The increased complexity of keeping track of thousands of people led our lead tech deacons, Jason and Chad, who both came to faith at the church, to research our options. They recommended to the elders a web portal technology that retails for around $800,000 and runs large corporations and state governments. After negotiating a lower price, we obtained the money from the sale of the old small church building and did not take the money from general tithes and offerings. I personally use technology just fine but cannot trouble-shoot anything beyond an Etch-A-Sketch. I won't try to explain the technology but will simply report that when we approved it, the tech guys started acting like Green Bay Packer fans after a playoff victory, so it must be good. We are hoping that it works so that we won't have to sell it for three dollars at a church garage sale.

More Facilities

Our current facility cannot accommodate much growth beyond our current four Sunday services. Additionally, our kids' ministry is bursting at the seams, our Capstone classes are in desperate need of space, and our cramped, windowless office space would be perfect if we were a third-world sweatshop.

So the elders voted to purchase a 43,000-square-foot dumpy warehouse Jamie found one block away from our current building. When the project is completed, we will have two buildings only a block apart, each hosting church services, with 1,300 seats in one location and a projected 1,000 seats in the other. We will be able to grow to more than 10,000 people per Sunday through multiple ser-vices in multiple locations. Each service will have live worship teams, but I will only be live in some services and on video in the others.

Some of our people are mildly unhappy about watching me preach on video instead of live because they feel it isn't very authen-tic. But in our current worship space, about half of the people sit so far away from the stage that they watch me on a video screen anyway.

Personally, I really like having the option of preaching only one sermon and videotaping it so that the rest of the day is covered in case of emergency. For example, I nearly didn't make it through a Sunday in the winter of 2005. I fell asleep on Saturday night and woke up at 1:00 a.m. with a flu bug that I had caught from my kids. That night, I ate a plate of nachos the size of a small Latin nation and spent the rest of the night throwing them up. I did not sleep for the rest of the night but did develop a nasty case of diarrhea, which left me dehydrated and exhausted.

The next day I felt that getting sent to hell would be an upgrade. I had managed to get about a combined hour of sleep between fluid launches out of various orifices like a human sprinkler. I preached with a barf bucket on the stage and told the sound guy that if I reached for the bucket, to turn my microphone off so that I did not barf over the sound system. My fear was that I would set off a chain reaction and turn our church into a neo-Roman vomitorium.

After the first service, a kind pharmacist brought me enough medications to piece me together, and it seemed I had a shot of actually making it through the day. Occasionally the barf would come up my throat, and I would just swallow hard and sort of eat it so that I could keep preaching, which was particularly delightful.

Knowing that I had four services to preach and that each sermon lasted about an hour, I was feeling optimistic during the third service — until I crapped myself about fifteen minutes into the sermon and was left with a terrible dilemma. Do I finish the sermon and just not move much on the stage? Do I say something spiritual, like the Holy Spirit just notified me that everyone is to break up into prayer groups, so I could sneak off and clean up the oil slick?

They don't cover this part of the job in seminary, and I was perplexed but chose to just keep going and finish the sermon, which took about another forty-five minutes, during which time I tried to breath out of my mouth to lessen the stench. This glorious day helped to convince me that videotaping the first sermon so that it could be shown at later services in case of emergency was a wise move.

More Parking

We have never had adequate parking in the history of our church, and the future appears to be no different. Parking has become our biggest dilemma to tackle.

More Security

As one of the largest churches in our state, we are a lightning rod for yahoos and various mixed nuts with an ax to grind or a desire to make the nightly news. Among them is a guy from Montana who hears voices telling him to take me out, which does not sound good. Without sounding paranoid, I also believe that larger churches are some of the softest potential terrorist targets in America. To make things safer, we have had to implement a security team in addition to having an off-duty police officer on-site.

More Training

I once read a pithy quote from Chuck Smith, who founded the Calvary Chapel movement. He said that most churches called the trained, but their churches trained the called. This simple distinction is profoundly important. The traditional model of ministry is that a person goes to seminary and is trained for ministry. Once they have completed their training and have passed their ordination exams, they are called into ministry by a church or denomination.

As Smith said, it is much wiser for someone to be overseen by leaders in a church who confirm that God has called them into ministry. Then, once their call has been confirmed, they should be trained by doing ministry in their church.

This point was reinforced by Dr. John Piper.[4] He encouraged me to make time for theological education and writing because each generation needs to define and defend Christian orthodoxy for themselves. His encouragement was wise and has helped me to validate in my own mind the need to make time for further education, study, and writing. So, though our church leaders nearly all began as new converts who were self-taught, our elders are now pursuing further education while working at Mars Hill, and I am finishing a degree at Western Seminary.

More Staff

In my conversations with pastors of large churches, the general rule of thumb seems to be that a staff member should be added to the church every time the Sunday attendance grows by roughly 130 to 150 people. We have in no way kept up with this pace and at times grow by as many as 500 people in one week for no discernable reason, which means that we are always understaffed.

We have always been reticent to add staff too quickly because we fear it may detract from the unpaid members of the church who are doing the ministry. We also do not want to hire prematurely in case our growth slows down, thereby leaving us financially short. We generally wait until a ministry had grown so large that a clear leader has emerged and then hire that person to expand the ministry. We have seen that this method of hiring also reduces our financial risk, since by the time we hire people, they have often grown such a large ministry that they have in effect raised their own salaries.

As we prepare for future growth, we have, however, identified some strategic hires that will need to be made, and we expect our staff to double within a year. One thing we still require of everyone we hire is a sense of awe and gratitude that they are privileged to work at Mars Hill and be a part of what God is doing by the power of his gospel. At this phase, we can't tolerate employees who are simply working a job.

More Money

In churches whose attendees are mostly young people, annual giving to the general fund is generally somewhere between $1,000 and $1,500 per adult of the average Sunday attendance. Therefore, a church comprised of largely young people that averages one hundred adults per Sunday should expect to have an annual general fund budget of roughly $100,000 to $150,000.

We have had to labor to train our people to work hard, budget wisely, invest smartly, spend carefully, and tithe generously. Pastor Jamie and a team of members, skilled in everything from life insurance to real estate and investing, conduct classes and seminars to teach our people how to be good stewards. Additionally, one week of our Gospel Class is devoted to the issue of stewardship.

We keep everyone informed via weekly email of exactly where we are at financially and have taken the subject of money and simply made it part of our church family discussions. For our people to own our mission, they also must own our expenses.

Getting young people to give regularly to their church has proven to be incredibly difficult across the nation. George Barna says, "Only 3 out of 10 twentysomethings donated to a church in the past year, which is half the proportion of older adults (30% to 61%). (While twentysomethings generally have smaller income levels than their older counterparts, this measure has nothing to do with how much the person donates, but whether they contribute financially at all to churches.) This reluctance to commit financially suggests that churches attracting an exclusively young adult audience will be especially hard-pressed to raise sufficient funds for ministry." [5]

At Mars Hill, the elders have chosen *not* to pass the offering plate during the church service. Instead, we offer people the following ways to give:

- We can set up a regularly scheduled deduction from their bank accounts.
- They can pay online via debit card.
- They can send a check to the office.
- They can put cash or a check in the offering boxes posted near the exits.
- They can place their gift in a basket when they come forward for communion each week.

About 60 percent of people who attend our church contribute financially to our church. The remaining 40 percent include many non-Christians, visitors, and people just checking us out. To make these people feel welcomed, we clearly state from the pulpit each week that if someone is a non-Christian or a visitor, we do *not* want them to give because they are our guests.

Although our members are roughly only 30 percent of our total Sunday attendance, they provide roughly 60 percent of our budget. And since we implemented an annual church member giving pledge some years ago, member giving has exceeded member pledges every year, and for the past few years, we have ended the budget year above budget. Our financial situation has greatly improved, as our weekly offering now surpasses the total offering that we received in our entire first year.

More Member Care

As the church grows, our pastors and leaders are getting swamped with new people who have very real and urgent needs because they are lost, addicted, perverted, and the like. It is probable that the waves of new people that keep pounding our shore will overwhelm our ability to care for both them and our existing church members.

So a large team of elders and deacons will use our new technology to track our members and ensure that they are connected, serving, giving, and in a learning and/or care group. In this way, we hope to preemptively help our members to live healthy and fruitful lives and avoid crises brought on by sin that went undetected for too long.

This means that it is vital to continually increase our small group ministry at a very rapid rate to keep up with the growth of the church. As we get bigger, we must also get smaller with hundreds of small home community groups, in which people will be known, loved, and sharing the gospel with lost friends.

Additionally, we are recording the Gospel Class and burning it on DVD to enable people to become members by watching the lectures in a home-based community group setting. This will allow us to raise up members wherever and whenever they can meet in small enough numbers for people to actually get to know one another instead of having everyone sit anonymously in a class of over four hundred people and wait for a personal interview at the end of the class.

More Church Planting

If you threw a dart at a map of Washington and did not hit water, a church plant is needed there because our state is among the least churched in the nation.[6] Honestly, I am glad that more people don't go to church in Seattle, because if they did, they would likely end up at churches led by pastors who are going to hell with their gay partners. Things are so bad that even two Baptist churches have gay pastors, and when the Baptists are gay, a city is officially lost. In the past decade, the greater Seattle area did see a net gain of 134 churches, but to keep up with the corresponding population growth, 456 more churches would have been needed in 2000.[7]

To help grow not only our church but also the wider church, we have brought on three full-time staff members to help with church planting because a church simply cannot be missional unless it is a church-planting church. We house the central office for the Acts 29 Network, which helps locate, assess, train, and deploy church planters around the nation and world, including over a dozen churches in our own region thus far. We give over 10 percent of our general giving to help support church planters because our prayer is to assist in the planting of one thousand churches.

More Kindness

When we started the church, I was full of pride, and by God's grace, I am now down to perhaps half a tank. I routinely critiqued the work of other men, particularly older men who had faithfully served Jesus by reaching modern and suburban types of people. It was typical young-buck-in-rutting-season folly.

But now that I've had a few years of ministry beatings, I am increasingly grateful for the Christian leaders whom Jesus is using even if they are considerably different from me. Over the years, I have had the unpleasant experience of being widely misunderstood, gossiped about, and criticized. For some reason, the perception has gotten out that I walk around with no pants on with a handgun in my underwear strap, drinking beer, eating meat, and screaming random verses out of the King James Bible.

Not knowing if I should respond to various wild rumors or ignore them, I sought the counsel of a more seasoned pastor. I emailed Rick Warren, assuming that he is now so big that he must wear a cup all the time just to get through an average day. He said that when your church is small, people ignore you; when your church is growing, people take credit for your success; and when your church gets big, people criticize and attack you. He then said the key was to simply remember that you work for an audience of one and to love everyone and not get off your mission of serving Jesus alone. His words rang true and convicted me to be kinder to other pastors who misunderstand what we are doing, because we are still one big dysfunctional church family under the same Father. To help build bridges of love and service to other local pastors, we now host a quarterly time of free training and networking over a meal, which is usually attended by over one hundred leaders from various churches.

More Pruning

It is my deepest desire to be fruitful for Jesus. And according to his frequent kingdom parables, fruit comes not simply by growing but by his strategic pruning. Jesus prunes us through hardship, suffering, failure, loss, discipline, and pain. I have found Jesus' pruning of my life, marriage, family, and church to be incredibly painful, but it always results in bigger, sweeter, and greater fruit. Some pruning has been so overwhelming that I did not know if I could endure it and even questioned the goodness of God despite my knowledge of Scripture, which led to bouts of despair and anger.

I wish I did not have to suffer demonic attacks that include seeing raw and real footage of the times my people were raped and molested that plays in my mind like a film even though I was not present. I wish I did not have to sometimes struggle so mightily to be intimate with my wife. I wish I did not feel so completely alone, especially when I am in a crowd. I wish I was not a target for critics who seem to put me on a pedestal only to get a better aim. I wish I did not have the responsibility of standing before God to give an account for the church that I lead. I wish I did not have to continually weep while watching people I dearly love shipwreck their faith and lives through folly, rebellion, sin, hard-heartedness, and deception. I wish I never had to climb on another airplane to go preach the gospel, because the picture of my children crying as I drive away haunts me while I am away from them. I wish I knew the future and how Jesus will prune me next so that I could wince to lessen its sting before the blow lands. But Jesus has called me to trust him by faith and to endure more pruning so that more fruit can be harvested for his kingdom. And for this reason, it is my deepest wish that Jesus keep pruning me, because I love him, want to be with him, want to be like him, and enjoy being on mission with him more than anything.

Thy kingdom come, thy will be done.

Amen.

Reformission Reflections

1. If you were to write a strategic plan for your church or ministry, how many people would you prepare for? What three things would you recommend stopping because they are not working? What three things would you recommend trying to begin?

2. How has God pruned your church or ministry in the past?

3. How is God pruning your church or ministry in the present?

4. In your opinion, what are the worst things the key leaders in your church or ministry suffer through?

5. Has your church or ministry ever helped to start a new church? What can be done to encourage your church or ministry to help start new churches that bring Jesus to lost people in your area and around the world?

6. Name one or two of the most painful seasons of pruning God has brought you through and the fruit that has resulted from those experiences.

7. What will you do differently now that you have read this book?

APPENDICES

The Junk Drawer

Answers to Common Questions

Why is there laughter in church at Mars Hill?

At Mars Hill, we take joy very seriously. Joy comes from God (Ps. 16:11), and joy makes us strong (Neh. 8:10). People who are close to God are filled with joy, and this joy enables them to get through the toils of life and laugh at the days to come like the wise woman in Proverbs 31:25. In Scripture, we see that Sarah laughed at the thought of getting pregnant in her old age (Gen. 18:13–15) and that God got the last laugh as Abraham and Sarah named their son Isaac, which means "laughter" (Gen. 21:1–6). We also see that there are times for laughter (Eccl. 3:4) and that sometimes the best thing to do is to laugh through our tears (Prov. 14:13). We also see the prophets and even Jesus using irony and sarcasm to convict people of sin and show how foolish sin is (e.g., Isa. 44:12–20; Matt. 19:24; 23:24). We also see that God laughs at the wicked, who in their folly disobey him to their own demise (Pss. 2:4; 37:13; 59:8). In summary, people are prone to taking themselves too seriously and God and their sin too lightly, so at Mars Hill, we use irony and sarcasm to learn to laugh at ourselves and to laugh with God because people are nuts and good comedic fodder.

Why does Mars Hill partake of communion every week?

In the early church, communion, also called the Lord's Supper, was accompanied by sincere introspection and repentance of one's sins (1 Cor. 11:17–34). During the first few years of our church, we did not partake of communion every week until we were studying the Passover from the book of Exodus and became convinced that it would be best to have the gospel of Jesus' death, burial, and resurrection for our sins as the center point of our church service to ensure that everyone was compelled to repentance of sin and faith in Jesus each week.

Why does Mars Hill sing songs I have never heard before?

The Bible tells us to sing "psalms, hymns and spiritual songs" (Eph. 5:19; Col. 3:16). And the Bible repeatedly tells us to sing new songs to the Lord (e.g., Pss. 33:3; 40:3; 144:9; 149:1; Isa. 42:10; Rev. 5:9; 14:3). Because God is our Creator who has made us in his image and likeness, it is important that we be creative. At Mars Hill, we enjoy singing from the Psalms, from other Scriptures that we set to music, older hymns that we have redone, as well as from a large library of songs that our own musicians have composed out of their love for God. Because of the richness of the resources God has given our church in the areas of songwriting and composition, we are blessed by an abundance of talent and creativity, for which we thank God and our artists.

How are children incorporated into worship at Mars Hill?

In the Old Testament when God's people would gather together, children were commonly included (Josh. 8:35; 2 Chron. 20:13; 31:16; Ezra 8:21; Neh. 8:2; 12:43). In the Old Testament, we see children commanded to worship God (Pss. 8:2; 148:12). We see Jesus as a child worshiping at the temple and learning with the adult men (Luke 2:46). In the time of Jesus, we also see children worshiping Jesus (Matt. 21:15–16), children being welcomed into his presence even though some adults felt they were a distraction to be kept away (Matt. 19:13–15), and Jesus telling us that we have a lot to learn from children (Matt. 18:1–6).

When children are quite young, it is admittedly difficult for them to sit through a church service, so we do provide a program during church for small children. This program includes age-appropriate prayer, Bible teaching, and worship. Our goal, however, is to have the children join the congregation for worship as young as possible, and we leave the timing of this up to the parents, although all children are encouraged to join us after the sermon for communion and worship no matter how young they are.

Why is no one speaking in tongues during the church service?

The issue of tongues is very controversial and divisive in many churches, and thankfully it has never been so at Mars Hill. The elders do not believe that the gift of tongues has ceased but believe that it is often not done in a biblical way. Mars Hill has leaders and members who speak in tongues, as well as leaders and members who do not. What Paul does forbid regarding tongues, however, is speaking in tongues out loud during a church service because visitors and non-Christians will not know what is being said, will think we are nutjobs, and would be better served by convicting Bible teaching so they can get saved (1 Cor. 14:12 – 25).

Are the Mars Hill pastors ordained?

The concept of ordination is man-made and finds no biblical backing in the Scriptures. Therefore, while the concept of ordination may not necessarily be bad, it is also not necessary. The closest thing we see in the New Testament to ordination is when the elders of a church laid hands on new leaders and commissioned them into church leadership (1 Tim. 4:14; 5:22). At Mars Hill, we do commission our new leaders into ministry by publicly laying hands on them and praying over them.

While the Bible does not require ordination, it does require that we obey the laws of our nation and state (Rom. 13:1 – 7). Our state government requires each church to license its pastors to do such things as conduct weddings, and Mars Hill follows these state laws and licenses each of our elder-pastors.

How are church leaders held accountable?

In an age of incredible sin among pastors, some of it very public and damaging to the reputation of Christianity, this is a vitally important question. At Mars Hill, we answer this question with a multi-layered answer.

First, an elder must fear God and be accountable to him. Simply, if any Christian, including a pastor, does not fear God and walk closely with Jesus by the power of the Holy Spirit, there is truly nothing that can be done to keep him or her from sin.

Second, an elder must be accountable to his wife if he is married. No one knows how a man is truly doing better than his wife, and an elder's wife must be an exemplary woman who helps her husband by speaking truthfully and respectfully to him about the condition of his heart and life.

Third, an elder must be accountable to the other elders. At Mars Hill, the elders are in close relationships of accountability. Our wives are also close to each other and are given the freedom to speak openly about the condition of their marriages and homes with one another so that sin among our elder team is difficult to hide.

Fourth, our elders are in relationship locally with a number of good Bible-teaching churches. Additionally, our elders are in relationship nationally with other pastors who are part of the Acts 29 Network.[1] We regularly speak and meet with many of these pastors, whom we love and with whom we have open, mutual accountability.

Fortunately, we have never had to discipline an elder for any sin because the closeness of our relationships brings potential issues to the surface before they manifest. Should an elder ever sin grievously, we would quickly discipline him according to the biblical directives (1 Tim. 5:19–21).

How does someone become an elder at Mars Hill?

The Bible teaches that it is God the Holy Spirit who ultimately selects the elders in the local church (Acts 20:28). Additionally, elders should not serve because of external compulsion (1 Peter 5:2), which is why we do not take congregational nominations for elders at Mars Hill. Instead, the Bible teaches that someone should become an elder because of internal compulsion given to them by God (1 Tim. 3:1; 1 Peter 5:2).

Practically, this means that someone desiring to be an elder at Mars Hill must first be a faithful member of the church. Then he speaks with one of the elders about his desire, and that elder assesses whether he is qualified for leadership according to the biblical criteria. If the elder does believe the man is qualified to be an elder, his nomination is brought before the entire group of elders, who must unanimously agree that the man is called of God and qualified to be brought through a slow process of testing (1 Tim. 3:10; 5:22). This process takes at least one year and requires that the potential candidate study, articulate in writing his doctrine and the area of ministry he hopes to lead, undergo an investigation of his family condition, and other things. After the lengthy process is concluded, the candidate is considered for eldership only if all the elders agree that he should be an elder. The elder candidate is then brought before the church, and if anyone should for any reason believe he is not qualified, we cancel his nomination if there are grounds to do so. If the man passes this lengthy process and is approved by the elders, deacons, and church members, he is then brought before the church with his family, and the elders lay hands and pray over him to commission him as an elder. Such men are generally still not paid to lead in the church, though at some point they may be employed by the church if the need arises.

How does someone become a deacon at Mars Hill?

Deacons are appointed by the elders and deacons according to the biblical qualifications and according to the needs of the church. The process of becoming a deacon is similar to that of an elder but takes less time to complete and is open to qualified women as well as men.

Do elders and deacons at Mars Hill serve terms?

We see no precedent in Scripture for placing time limitations on our leaders (e.g., three-year terms). Additionally, serving terms causes turnover, which makes for discontinuity in decision-making and oversights because projects, people, and needs in the church do not magically go away every three years to allow new leaders to take over.

Our elders are expected to give their lives to service in our church unless they are called by God to serve elsewhere, they should disqualify themselves in some way, or they are simply unable to perform their duties due to such reasons as health. We do, however, grant elders seasons of Sabbath as needed.

Some deacons are appointed to specific tasks, and so once their task is completed, they do not continue as a deacon unless they are assigned to another task. Some deacons serve until life circumstances such as marriage, the birth of a child, or a move require them to step down as deacons. Still other deacons are overseeing areas of ministry that are ongoing and will remain in their position indefinitely.

What should someone do if they disagree with how Mars Hill is led?

We encourage those who may disagree with us to a significant degree to examine all their beliefs regarding church government by studying Scripture because we are convinced that our church is operating according to the principles of the Bible.

If, after serious study, they should disagree with us to the degree that they cannot submit to our leaders and operate within our church structures, we encourage them to find a church in which they can participate with a clear conscience. If their differences are relatively minor, or if they can respect our church leaders and structures without being divisive, we welcome them to stay at Mars Hill.

Distinctives of Larger Churches

Larger churches have a different kind of pastor

* The preaching pastor has a long tenure, is funny, and preaches well.

* The preaching pastor mainly preaches and does not do much counseling.

* The preaching pastor is not as accessible as a pastor of a small church.

* The preaching pastor understands how to raise large sums of money when needed.

* The preaching pastor works well with the media to increase church exposure.

* The preaching pastor learns from other pastors of large churches, not from conferences.

Larger churches are led differently

* Larger churches are able to make decisions with the involvement of fewer people.

* Larger churches are able to shape their direction with the involvement of fewer people.

* Larger churches have multiple leadership teams instead of one team.

* Larger churches hire specialists with narrow ministry areas, not generalists.

- Larger churches have multiple levels of organizational responsibility and multiple centers of organizational leadership and are not run by the primary leader.
- Larger churches hire more from within the church than do smaller churches.
- Larger churches hire slowly and fire quickly.
- Larger churches must plan much further ahead because they are more complicated.

Larger churches use their facilities differently

- Larger churches tend to have longer worship services than smaller congregations do.
- Larger churches are willing to open their doors as often as is needed to grow.
- Larger churches depend on small groups in homes, whereas smaller churches conduct most of their church meetings in the church building.

Larger churches have higher expectations

- Larger churches have higher expectations for their members' active participation.
- Larger churches have a higher number of higher-quality ministries and expect a higher level of excellence than do comparable ministries in smaller churches.
- Larger churches expect to lose people who are not committed to their mission, while smaller churches work much harder at keeping people from leaving the church.
- Larger churches generally have a superior music ministry.

Larger churches rely more on their own resources

● Larger churches function independently or in loosely affiliated networks.

● Local leaders govern larger churches, while smaller churches rely more on regional or national leadership.

● Larger churches are more likely to plant churches or to have multiple sites.

● Larger churches innovate new ministries, and smaller churches copy successful models from other churches.

Larger churches are theologically conservative and culturally liberal

● Larger churches tend to be more conservative in theology and more liberal in practice, while smaller churches are often more liberal in theology (e.g., denial of eternal hell) and conservative in practice (e.g., liturgy, hymns, vestments).

● Larger churches tend to present clear, authoritative teaching from Scripture, while theological pluralism tends to thrive in smaller churches.

Notes

Prelude

1. Cathy Lynn Gossman, "Charting the Unchurched in America," *USA Today*, March 7, 2002, www.usatoday.com/life/2002/2002-03-07-no-religion.htm (accessed June 21, 2005); Theron Zahn, "Washington State May Be Losing Its Faith," *KOMO News*, March 17, 2002, www.komotv.com/news/story_m.asp?ID=17365 (accessed June 21, 2005); David T. Olson, *The State of the Church in the Seattle Metro Area 1990–2000*, CD-ROM (2004), slides 16, 18. Olson's CD can be purchased from The American Church, www.theamericanchurch.org/metro.htm.
2. John N. Vaughan, "Learning from America's Top 100 Fastest-Growing Churches," *Outreach*, July–August 2005, 51–56; John N. Vaughan, "Top 50 Most Influential Churches," *The Church Report*, July 2005, www.thechurchreport. com/content/view/484/32/.
3. George Barna, "Twentysomethings Struggle to Find Their Place in Christian Churches," *The Barna Update*, September 24, 2003, The Barna Group, www.barna. org/FlexPage.aspx?Page=BarnaUpdate&BarnaUpdateID=149.
4. Ibid.
5. George Barna, "Church Attendance," *Barna by Topic*, 2005, The Barna Group, www.barna.org/FlexPage.aspx?Page=Topic&TopicID=10.
6. John N. Vaughan, *America's Megachurches 2005*, CD-ROM version 5.1 (Church Growth Today, 2005), slide 215. This PowerPoint seminar CD can be purchased from Church Growth Today, www.churchgrowthtoday.com/Content/ContentCT. asp?P=19.
7. Barna, "Church Attendance."
8. Richard Florida, *The Rise of the Creative Class: And How It's Transforming Work, Leisure, Community and Everyday Life* (New York: Basic, 2002).
9. William H. Frey, "Generational Pull," *American Demographics* 26, no. 4 (May 2004): 18–19. William Frey is a demographer at the Brookings Institution and a research professor at the University of Michigan Population Studies Center. His website is www.frey-demographer.org. Also see "Seattle Area a Big Draw for College-Educated Singles," *Puget Sound Business Journal*, November 3, 2003.
10. Ibid.
11. Ibid.

Chapter Zero: Ten Curious Questions

1. Mark Driscoll, *The Radical Reformission: Reaching Out without Selling Out* (Grand Rapids: Zondervan, 2004).
2. The following discussion and the categories of traditional and institutional, contemporary and evangelical, and emerging and missional churches summarizes the work and ideas of Scott Thomas, who is a friend, an Acts 29 board member, and the pastor of the Encounter Church in Colorado (www.encounterchurch.com).
3. Lyle Schaller, *The Very Large Church* (Nashville: Abingdon, 2000), 53.

4. Ibid. See also Robert D. Putnam, *Bowling Alone: The Collapse and Revival of American Community* (New York: Simon and Schuster, 2000), 76.

5. Dan Kimball, *The Emerging Church* (Grand Rapids: Zondervan, 2003).

6. For an example of this position, see Joel B. Green and Mark D. Baker (whom I affectionately refer to as Hymenaus and Alexander), *Recovering the Scandal of the Cross: Atonement in New Testament and Contemporary Contexts* (Downers Grove, IL: InterVarsity Press, 2000); as well as Brian D. McLaren, *A Generous Orthodoxy* (Grand Rapids: Zondervan, 2004), 45–49. For those readers who wish to grow in their understanding of what Jesus accomplished by dying in our place and rising from the dead, I recommend John Piper, *Counted Righteous in Christ: Should We Abandon the Imputation of Christ's Righteousness?* (Wheaton, IL: Crossway, 2002); Alister E. McGrath, *What Was God Doing on the Cross?* (Grand Rapids: Zondervan, 1993); Leon Morris, *The Atonement: Its Meaning and Significance* (Downers Grove, IL: InterVarsity Press, 1983); John Murray, *Redemption Accomplished and Applied* (Grand Rapids: Eerdmans, 1955); John R. W. Stott, *The Cross of Christ* (Downers Grove, IL: InterVarsity Press, 1986); and Bruce Demarest, ed., *The Cross and Salvation* (Wheaton, IL: Crossway, 1997).

7. A pioneering work for the pro-gay and "Christian" position is John Boswell, *Christianity, Social Tolerance, and Homosexuality: Gay People in Western Europe from the Beginning of the Christian Era to the Fourteenth Century* (Chicago: University of Chicago Press, 1980). Another pro-gay and "Christian" book of note is Mel White, *Stranger at the Gate: To Be Gay and Christian in America* (New York: Penguin, 1994), in which he tells of his secret life as a gay man while acting as a powerful evangelical Christian. For a biblical position on homosexuality, a good read is Robert A. J. Gagnon, *The Bible and Homosexual Practice* (Nashville: Abingdon, 2002), as well as his website, www.robgagnon.net. Joseph Nicolosi provides clinical insights on the issue in *Reparative Therapy of Male Homosexuality: A New Clinical Approach* (Northvale, NJ: Jason Aronson, 1991). For good preventive insights, see Jason Nicolosi and Linda Ames Nicolosi, *A Parent's Guide to Preventing Homosexuality* (Downers Grove, IL: InterVarsity Press, 2002). Perhaps the saddest example of the Emergent answer to the question of homosexuality was given by Brian McLaren in the *Time* magazine cover story "The 25 Most Influential Evangelicals in America," (February 7, 2005): "Asked at a conference last spring what he thought about gay marriage, Brian McLaren replied, 'You know what, the thing that breaks my heart is that there's no way I can answer it without hurting someone on either side'" (45). Sadly, by failing to answer, McLaren was unwilling to say what the Bible says.

8. For example, see Brian D. McLaren, *The Last Word and the Word after That: A Tale of Faith, Doubt, and a New Kind of Christianity* (San Francisco: Jossey-Bass, 2005). To better understand the biblical doctrine of hell, see Robert A. Peterson, *Hell On Trial: The Case for Eternal Punishment* (Phillipsburg, NJ: P & R, 1995); Douglas J. Moo, *Hell under Fire: Modern Scholarship Reinvents Eternal Punishment* (Grand Rapids: Zondervan, 2004); David George Moore, *The Battle for Hell* (Lanham, MD: Univ. Press of America, 1996); Harry Buis, *The Doctrine of Eternal Punishment* (Philadelphia: Presbyterian and Reformed, 1957); and John H. Gerstner, *Repent or Perish: A Biblical Response to the Conservative Attack on Hell* (Ligonier, PA: Soli Deo Gloria, 1990). Or just read the words of Jesus in the gospels, since he spoke about hell more than anyone.

9. For example, see Gregory A. Boyd, *God of the Possible: A Biblical Introduction to the Open View of God* (Grand Rapids: Baker, 2000); Clark Pinnock et al., *The Openness of God* (Downers Grove, IL: InterVarsity Press, 1994); John Sanders, *The God Who Risks: A Theology of Providence* (Downers Grove, IL: InterVarsity Press, 1998); and Clark Pinnock, *Most Moved Mover: A Theology of God's Openness* (Grand Rapids: Baker Academic, 2001). To get a biblical view of God's foreknowledge of and rule over the future, see Bruce A. Ware, *God's Lesser Glory: The Diminished God of Open Theism* (Wheaton, IL: Crossway, 2000); John Piper, Justin Taylor, and Paul Kjoss Helseth, eds., *Beyond the Bounds: Open Theism and the Undermining of Biblical Christianity* (Wheaton, IL: Crossway, 2003); Bruce A. Ware, *Their God Is Too Small: Open Theism and the Undermining of Confidence in God* (Wheaton, IL: Crossway, 2003); John M. Frame, *No Other God: A Response to Open Theism* (Phillipsburg, NJ: P & R, 2001); Douglas Wilson, ed., *Bound Only Once: The Failure of Open Theism* (Moscow, ID: Canon, 2001); Millard J. Erickson, *What Does God Know and When Does He Know It? The Current Controversy over Divine Foreknowledge* (Grand Rapids: Zondervan, 2003); and H. Wayne House, *Charts on Open Theism and Orthodoxy* (Grand Rapids: Kregel, 2004).

10. For example, see William J. Webb, *Slaves, Women and Homosexuals: Exploring the Hermeneutics of Cultural Analysis* (Downers Grove, IL: InterVarsity Press, 2001). To get a better perspective on this issue, I recommend John Piper and Wayne Grudem, eds., *Recovering Biblical Manhood and Womanhood: A Response to Evangelical Feminism* (Wheaton, IL: Crossway, 1991).

11. For example, see McLaren, *A Generous Orthodoxy*, 74–75. For a biblical position, see D. A. Carson, *The Inclusive-Language Debate: A Plea for Realism* (Grand Rapids: Baker, 1998); and Vern S. Poythress and Wayne A. Grudem, *The TNIV and the Gender-Neutral Bible Controversy* (Nashville: Broadman and Holman, 2004).

12. For a good understanding of the current confusion over how to read and interpret Scripture, Kevin J. Vanhoozer, *Is There a Meaning in This Text?* (Grand Rapids: Zondervan, 1998) is helpful, as well as his *First Theology: God, Scriptures and Hermeneutics* (Downers Grove, IL: InterVarsity Press, 2002).

13. Abraham H. Maslow, *Motivation and Personality*, 3rd ed. (New York: HarperCollins, 1987).

14. Perhaps the most popular book espousing the gospel of self-esteem is Joel Osteen, *Your Best Life Now: Seven Steps to Living at Your Full Potential* (New York: Warner Faith, 2004).

15. Michael Frost and Alan Hirsch, *The Shaping of Things to Come* (Peabody, MA: Hendrickson, 2003) has become quite popular among younger and more missionally minded Christians. However, while the book is very strong on the incarnational aspect of Jesus' ministry, it altogether ignores his attractional ministries, such as teaching and performing miracles.

16. John N. Vaughan, *America's Megachurches 2005*, CD-ROM version 5.1 (Church Growth Today, 2005), slides 18, 20, 51; Schaller, *The Very Large Church*, 17, 28, 43–45; George Barna, "Small Churches Struggle to Grow Because of the People They Attract," *The Barna Update*, September 2, 2003, The Barna Group, www.barna.org/FlexPage.aspx?Page=BarnaUpdate&BarnaUpdateID=148 (accessed June 21, 2005).

17. Vaughan, *America's Megachurches 2005*, slide 51; "About Us," *Church Growth Today*: www.churchgrowthtoday.com/Content/ContentCT.asp?P=19 (June 21, 2005).

18. In a footnote to his book *Bowling Alone*, Robert Putnam writes, "See C. Kirk Hadaway, Penny Long Marler, and Mark Chaves, 'What the Polls Don't Show: A Closer Look at U.S. Church Attendance,' *American Sociological Review* 58 (December 1993): 741–52; Mark Chaves and James C. Cavendish, 'More Evidence on U.S. Catholic Church Attendance,' *Journal for the Scientific Study of Religion* 33 (December 1994): 376–81; and 'Symposium: Surveys of U.S. Church Attendance.' According to the 1996 General Social Survey, only 2 percent of people who did not attend church 'last week' report that they attended some *other* type of religious event or meeting. Thus the standard question does not 'miss' a significant number of people who attend, say, prayer meetings *instead of* church services" (Putnam, *Bowling Alone*, 453n. 29). Also see David T. Olson, *Ten Fascinating Facts about the American Church*, CD-ROM (2004), slide 3, *The American Church*: www.TheAmericanChurch.org.

19. Barna, "Small Churches Struggle."

20. Schaller, *The Very Large Church*, 42.

21. Barna, "Small Churches Struggle."

22. John N. Vaughan, *Megachurches and America's Cities: How Churches Grow* (Bolivar, MS: Church Growth Today, 2003), 19. Lyle Schaller defines a megachurch as any church with a weekly attendance of adults and children that is at least 1,801 people (*The Very Large Church*, 28).

23. Vaughan, *Megachurches and America's Cities*, 24. For those wanting to learn more about Spurgeon, see Lewis A. Drummond, *Spurgeon: Prince of Preachers* (Grand Rapids: Kregel, 1992); Iain H. Murray, *The Forgotten Spurgeon* (Carlisle, PN: Banner of Truth, 1966); Iain H. Murray, *Spurgeon V Hyper-Calvinism: The Battle for Gospel Preaching* (Carlisle, PN: Banner of Truth, 1995); Eric Hayden, *The Unforgettable Spurgeon* (Greenville, SC: Emerald House Group, 1997); and Arnold Dallimore, *Spurgeon: A New Biography* (Carlisle, PN: Banner of Truth, 1995).

24. Vaughan, *Megachurches and America's Cities*, 24.

25. Elmer Towns, *The Ten Largest Sunday Schools* (Grand Rapids: Baker, 1969).

26. Vaughan, *America's Megachurches 2005* (version 5.2), slide 38.

27. Schaller, *The Very Large Church*, 16–17.

28. Michael Frost and Alan Hirsch, *The Shaping of Things to Come* (Peabody, MA: Hendrickson, 2003).

29. Thomas F. Mathews, *The Early Churches of Constantinople: Architecture and Liturgy* (University Park, PN: Pennsylvania State University Press, 1971); Vaughan, *Megachurches and America's Cities*, 24; and John N. Vaughan, *The Large Church: A Twentieth-Century Expression of the First-Century Church* (Grand Rapids: Baker, 1985), 33–43.

30. Vaughan, *America's Megachurches 2005*, slides 54–55.

31. "Yoido Full Gospel Church Story," Full Gospel Television, http://english.fgtv.com/yfgc.pdf (accessed June 21, 2005).

32. Craig Keener, Larry Osborne, and Mark Driscoll, "An Army of Ones," *Leadership* 26, no. 2 (Spring 2005): 38–43.

33. Peter M. Senge, *The Fifth Discipline: The Art and Practice of the Learning Organization* (New York: Currency, 1994), 341–45.

34. To better understand these concepts, see Stephen R. Covey et al., *First Things First: To Live, to Love, to Learn, to Leave a Legacy* (New York: Simon and Schuster, 1994).

35. I took the concept of shooting our dogs from a conversation I had with a friend named Jon Phelps, who is the president of DC–3 Entertainment and the founder of Full Sail College.

Chapter One: Jesus, Our Offering Was $137 and I Want to Use It to Buy Bullets

1. I took this punch line from a stand-up comedian I heard while flipping through the channels one night; the comedian's name remains unknown to me.

2. The concept of organizational infancy was taken from Michael E. Gerber, *The E-Myth Revisited: Why Most Small Businesses Don't Work and What to Do about It*, 2nd ed. (New York: HarperCollins, 2001).

3. This chart is adapted from Frost and Hirsch, *The Shaping of Things to Come*, with two major changes. First, they placed missiology above ecclesiology in the order of priority, which diminishes the importance of biblical church leadership to define and lead the mission. Second, I added the fourth category of ministry so that each individual Christian would be aware that their ministry service is their way of serving Jesus under their church leaders as part of the mission of a local church.

4. For further study on principles for organizing church leadership, see Gene A. Getz, *Elders and Leaders: God's Plan for Leading the Church* (Chicago: Moody Publishers, 2003); on the biblical teaching on pastors-elders, see Alexander Strauch, *Biblical Eldership: An Urgent Call to Restore Biblical Church Leadership* (Littleton, CO: Lewis and Roth, 1995); on church priorities, see Mark Dever, *Nine Marks of a Healthy Church* (Wheaton, IL: Crossway, 2004); for practical principles on cultivating an effective leadership team, see Larry W. Osborne, *The Unity Factor: Developing a Healthy Church Leadership Team*, 3rd ed. (Vista, CA: Owl's Nest, 2001); and for insights on being a godly pastor, see Richard Baxter, *The Reformed Pastor* (Carlisle, PA: Banner of Truth, 1979), and Eugene H. Peterson, *The Contemplative Pastor: Returning to the Art of Spiritual Direction* (Grand Rapids: Eerdmans, 1989).

Chapter Two: Jesus, If Anyone Else Calls My House, I May Be Seeing You Real Soon

1. Vanessa Ho, "Just 33 Percent in State Attend Church, Yet Some Faiths Are Thriving," *Seattle Post-Intelligencer*, September 19, 2002, http://seattlepi.nwsource.com/local/87669_religion19.shtml?searchpagefrom=1&searchdiff=1014; Patricia O'Connell Killen, *Religion and Public Life in the Pacific Northwest: The None Zone* (Lanham, MD: AltaMira, 2004); "Kidless in Seattle," *Seattle Times*, 2000, http://seattletimes.nwsource.com/art/census2000/charts/censuschildrenchart08.pdf; "Where the Children Live," *Seattle Times*, 2000, http://seattletimes.nwsource.com/art/census2000/maps/kidsregionalmap08.pdf; and "Children in Seattle," *Seattle Times*, 2000, http://seattletimes.nwsource.com/art/census2000/charts/childrenpopulation08.pdf.

2. Timothy Egan, "Vibrant Cities Find One Thing Missing: Children," *New York Times*, March 24, 2005, A1. (Also available at www.nytimes.com/2005/03/24/national/24childless.html.)

3. I gained a lot from R. Bruce Bickel, *Light and Heat: A Puritan View of the Pulpit* (Ligonier, PA: Soli Deo Gloria, 1999); William Perkins, *The Art of Prophesying* (Carlisle, PA: Banner of Truth, 1996); D. Martyn Lloyd-Jones, *Preaching and Preachers* (Grand Rapids: Zondervan, 1971); and Martin Luther, *Lectures on Galatians* (St. Louis: Concordia, 1963), which is different from his commentary on Galatians and greatly helped to clarify that the gospel is about who you love and not just about what you do.

Chapter Four: Jesus, Could You Please Rapture the Charismaniac Lady Who Brings Her Tambourine to Church?

1. Malcolm Gladwell, *The Tipping Point: How Little Things Can Make a Big Difference* (New York: Back Bay, 2002), 179.
2. Ibid., 172–73.
3. Ibid., 180.
4. Ibid., 180–81.
5. The concept of organizational adolescence is taken from Gerber, *The E-Myth Revisited*.
6. Donald Miller, *Blue Like Jazz: Nonreligious Thoughts on Christian Spirituality* (Nashville: Thomas Nelson, 2003); Donald Miller, *Searching for God Knows What* (Nashville: Thomas Nelson, 2004); Donald Miller, *Prayer and the Art of Volkswagen Maintenance* (Eugene, OR: Harvest House, 2000).
7. Chris Seay, *The Gospel According to Tony Soprano: An Unauthorized Look Into the Soul of TV's Top Mob Boss and His Family* (New York: Jeremy P. Tarcher, 2002); Chris Seay, *Faith of My Fathers: Conversations with Three Generations of Pastors about Church, Ministry, and Culture* (Grand Rapids: Zondervan, 2005); and Chris Seay and Chad Karger, *To Become One: After "I Do," The Real Journey Begins* (Lake Mary, FL: Relevant, 2004).
8. Recordings of the David Crowder Band include *All I Can Say*, compact disc (Independent: July 1, 1998); *Can You Hear Us?* compact disc (Sparrow/Emd: February 26, 2002); *Illuminate*, compact disc (Sparrow/Emd: September 16, 2003); *The Lime CD*, compact disc (Sparrow/Emd: March 23, 2004); *Sunsets and Sushi*, compact disc (Sparrow/Emd: February 15, 2005).
9. Dan Kimball, *The Emerging Church* (Grand Rapids: Zondervan, 2003); Dan Kimball, *Emerging Worship: Creating Worship Gatherings for New Generations* (Grand Rapids: Zondervan, 2004).
10. In an effort to understand postmodernism, I started by studying René Descartes and his view of knowledge and truth. I then studied a great deal on Blaise Pascal, a contemporary of Descartes who disagreed with his epistemology and foresaw the implications of Descartes' errors, which led to rationalism, deism, and eventually atheism. A simple introduction to Pascal is Thomas V. Morris, *Making Sense of It All: Pascal and the Meaning of Life* (Grand Rapids: Eerdmans, 1992); and helpful in understanding Pascal's alternative to Descartes, if you can overlook the author's Catholic biases at the end of the book, is Peter Kreeft, *Christianity for Modern Pagans: Pascal's Pensées* (San Francisco: Ignatius Press, 1993). To better understand some of the foundational thinkers of postmodernity, I read up on Frederick Nietzsche and Martin Heidegger, including James L. Perotti, *Heidegger on the*

Divine: The Thinker, the Poet, and God (Athens, OH: Ohio University Press, 1974), in an effort to figure out Heidegger's complex view of God. I also looked at the history of modern philosophy by reading Frederick C. Copleston, *A History of Philosophy*, vol. 4 (New York: Image, 1994); and Gordon Michalson, *Lessing's 'Ugly Ditch': A Study of Theology and History* (University Park, PA: Pennsylvania State University Press, 1985). I tried to wade through some of the postmodern thinkers, especially the more spiritually focused books: John D. Caputo and Michael J. Scanlon, eds., *God, the Gift, and Postmodernism* (Bloomington, IN: Indiana University Press, 1999); Jacques Derrida and John D. Caputo, *Deconstruction in a Nutshell: A Converstaion with Jacques Derrida* (Bronx: Fordham University Press, 1997); and Jacques Derrida, *The Gift of Death* (Chicago: University of Chicago Press, 1995). I read some overviews of postmodernism, including Zygmunt Bauman, *Postmodernity and Its Discontents* (New York: New York University Press, 1997); Huston Smith, *Beyond the Post-Modern Mind* (Wheaton, IL: Quest, 1989); Anthony C. Thiselton, *Interpreting God and the Postmodern Self: On Meaning, Manipulation and Promise* (Grand Rapids: Eerdmans, 1995); Paul Lakeland, *Postmodernity: Christian Identity in a Fragmented Age* (Minneapolis: Augsburg Fortress, 1997); and Craig Kennet Miller, *Postmoderns: The Beliefs, Hopes, and Fears of Young Americans Born 1965–1981* (Nashville: Discipleship Resources, 1996). I then investigated the implications of postmodernism: on truth, Walter Truett Anderson, ed., *The Truth about the Truth* (New York: Jeremy P. Tarcher/Putnam, 1995); on understanding, Michael Polanyi and Harry Prosch, *Meaning* (Chicago: University of Chicago Press, 1975); on leadership, Margaret J. Wheatley, *Leadership and the New Science: Discovering Order in a Chaotic World* (San Francisco: Berret-Koehler, 1999); on morality and ethics, Edith Wyschogrod, *Saints and Postmodernism: Revisioning Moral Philosophy* (Chicago: University of Chicago Press, 1990); and on the social sciences, David R. Dickens and Andrea Fontana, eds., *Postmodernism and Social Inquiry* (New York: Guilford, 1994). I then looked at how the transition from modernism to postmodernism might be part of a larger historical shift: William Strauss and Neil Howe, *The Fourth Turning: An American Prophecy* (New York: Broadway, 1997). And I examined the role of Christianity in the postmodern world: Stanley Hauerwas, *After Christendom? How the Church Is to Behave If Freedom, Justice, and a Christian Nation Are Bad Ideas* (Nashville: Abingdon, 1991); Stanley Hauerwas and William H. Willimon, *Resident Aliens: Life in the Christian Colony* (Nashville: Abingdon, 1989); and Rodney Clapp, *A Peculiar People: The Church as Culture in a Post-Christian Society* (Downers Grove, IL: InterVarsity Press, 1996). I looked at some of the early critiques of modern faith: J. Gresham Machen, *Christianity and Liberalism* (Grand Rapids: Eerdmans, 1923); and I looked at the works of Francis A. Schaeffer, particularly *The Church at the End of the Twentieth Century* (Downers Grove, IL: InterVarsity Press, 1970). I also read evangelical Christian explanations of postmodernism: Stanley J. Grenz, *A Primer on Postmodernism* (Grand Rapids: Eerdmans, 1996); and Gene Edward Veith Jr., *Postmodern Times: A Christian Guide to Contemporary Thought and Culture* (Wheaton, IL: Crossway, 1994). I also investigated some Christian critiques of postmodernism, such as D. A. Carson, *The Gagging of God: Christianity Confronts Pluralism* (Grand Rapids: Zondervan, 1996); Dennis McCallum, ed., *The Death of*

Truth: Responding to Multiculturalism, the Rejection of Reason and the New Postmodern Diversity (Minneapolis: Bethany House, 1996); and Alister McGrath, *A Passion for Truth: The Intellectual Coherence of Evangelicalism* (Downers Grove, IL: InterVarsity Press, 1996). I then examined the emerging postmodern critique of foundational theology: Nancey Murphy, *Beyond Liberalism and Fundamentalism: How Modern and Postmodern Philosophy Set the Theological Agenda* (Harrisburg, PA: Trinity Press International, 1996). And I examined the attempt at post-foundational theology: George A. Lindbeck, *The Nature of Doctrine: Religion and Theology in a Postliberal Age* (Philadelphia: Westminster/John Knox, 1984); and Timothy R. Phillips and Dennis L. Okholm, eds., *The Nature of Confession: Evangelicals and Postliberals in Conversation* (Downers Grove, IL: InterVarsity Press, 1996). I also looked at the trend in Great Britain of Christians embracing postmodernity: Dave Tomlinson, *The Post-Evangelical* (Grand Rapids: Zondervan, 2003); and Graham Cray, *Post-Evangelical Debate* (London: SPCK, 2000). Lastly, I examined a missional approach to reaching postmodern people: Lesslie Newbigin, *The Gospel in a Pluralist Society* (Grand Rapids: Eerdmans, 1989). All of this to simply say that in the mid and late 1990s, this is how a lot of my free time was spent, and in the end, after muttering 1 Corinthians 1:20–21 — "Where is the wise man? Where is the scholar? Where is the philosopher of this age? Has not God made foolish the wisdom of the world? For since in the wisdom of God the world through its wisdom did not know him, God was pleased through the foolishness of what was preached to save those who believe." — I simply moved on to preach the bloody death and triumphant victory of Jesus. For my fellow young Christian pastors prone to jump on faddish bandwagons like I did, I would simply urge you to at least do your homework and see if you can find anyone wiser than Jesus to found your life and ministry on. If not, just stick with him.

11. Max Picard, *The Flight from God* (Washington, D.C.: Regnery Gateway, 1989).
12. Doug Pagitt, *Preaching Re-Imagined: The Role of the Sermon in Communities of Faith* (Grand Rapids: Zondervan, 2005); Doug Pagitt, *Reimagining Spiritual Formation: A Week in the Life of an Experimental Church* (Grand Rapids: Zondervan, 2003).
13. Books by Brian McLaren include: *Finding Faith: A Self-Discovery Guide for Your Spiritual Quest* (Grand Rapids: Zondervan, 1999); *A New Kind of Christian: A Tale of Two Friends on a Spiritual Journey* (San Francisco: Jossey-Bass, 2001); *More Ready Than You Realize: Evangelism as Dance in the Postmodern Matrix* (Grand Rapids: Zondervan, 2002); *The Story We Find Ourselves In: Further Adventures of a New Kind of Christian* (San Francisco: Jossey-Bass, 2003); *The Church on the Other Side: Doing Ministry in the Postmodern Matrix* (Grand Rapids: Zondervan, 2003); and *A Generous Orthodoxy* and *The Last Word and the Word after That* (cited earlier). Books he has coauthored include: Brian D. McLaren and Tony Campolo, *Adventures in Missing the Point: How the Culture-Controlled Church Neutered the Gospel* (Grand Rapids: Zondervan, 2003); and Leonard Sweet, Brian D. McLaren, and Jerry Haselmayer, *A is for Abductive: The Language of the Emerging Church* (Grand Rapids: Zondervan, 2003).
14. See www.emergentvillage.com for more information.
15. Rick Warren, *The Purpose-Driven Church: Growth without Compromising Your Message and Mission* (Grand Rapids: Zondervan, 1995).

16. See www.gocn.org; Darrell L. Guder, *The Continuing Conversion of the Church* (Grand Rapids: Eerdmans, 2000); Darrell L. Guder, ed., *Missional Church: A Vision for the Sending of the Church in North America* (Grand Rapids: Eerdmans, 1998); George R. Hunsberger and Craig Van Gelder, eds., *The Church between Gospel and Culture: The Emerging Mission in North America* (Grand Rapids: Eerdmans, 1996).

17. Alan J. Roxburgh, *The Missionary Congregation, Leadership, and Liminality* (Harrisburg, PA: Trinity Press International, 1997); Alan J. Roxburgh, "Missional Leadership: Equipping God's People for Mission," in *Missional Church*, ed. Darrell L. Guder (Grand Rapids: Eerdmans, 1998), 183–220.

18. For further study on this subject, see James R. Beck and Craig L. Blomberg, eds., *Two Views on Women in Ministry* (Grand Rapids: Zondervan, 2001). My position is essentially the one proposed by Blomberg in the appendix.

19. To more thoroughly think through this and other methods for improving steward-ship in your church, see George Barna, *How to Increase Giving at Your Church: A Practical Guide to the Sensitive Task of Raising Money for Your Church or Ministry* (Ventura, CA: Regal Books 1997).

Chapter Five: Jesus, Why Am I Getting Fatter and Meaner?

1. Helpful books on the demonic include: as a good introduction to spiritual warfare, Charles Spurgeon, *Spiritual Warfare in a Believer's Life*, ed. Robert Hall (Seattle: YWAM, 1993); for practical insights, C. S. Lewis, *The Screwtape Letters* (New York: Macmillan, 1961); for pastoral help, Neil T. Anderson, *The Bondage Breaker*, 2nd ed. (Eugene, OR: Harvest House, 2000); on demonic temptation to sin, Thomas Brooks, *Precious Remedies against Satan's Devices* (Carlisle, PA: Banner of Truth, 1984); on demonization, C. Fred Dickason, *Demon Possession and the Christian* (Wheaton, IL: Crossway, 1987); for an overview of biblical texts on the issue, Edward F. Murphy, *The Handbook for Spiritual Warfare* (Nashville: Thomas Nelson, 2003); and for an examination of Paul's dealings with Satan and demons, Clinton E. Arnold, *Power and Magic: The Concept of Power in Ephesians* (Eugene, OR: Wipf and Stock, 2001), and Clinton E. Arnold, *Powers of Darkness: Principalities and Powers in Paul's Letters* (Downers Grove, IL: InterVarsity Press, 1992).

Chapter Six: Jesus, Today We Voted to Take a Jackhammer to Your Big Church

1. The concept of organizational comfort is adapted from Gerber, *The E-Myth Revisited.*

2. Acts 29 is the church-planting network of which I am president. For more informa-tion, visit www.Acts29Network.org.

3. Vaughan, *Megachurches and America's Cities*, 99.

4. See Schaller, *The Very Large Church*; Vaughan, *Megachurches and America's Cities*; Carl F. George, *How to Break Growth Barriers: Capturing Overlooked Opportuni-ties for Church Growth* (Grand Rapids: Baker, 1993); Gary L. McIntosh, *One Size Doesn't Fit All: Bringing Out the Best in Any Size Church* (Grand Rapids: Baker, 1999); Lyle E. Schaller, *The Multiple Staff and the Larger Church* (Nashville: Abing-don, 1980); Barna, "Small Churches Struggle"; and Church Growth Today, www. churchgrowthtoday.com, for many resources. For those who are interested, some

of the more pertinent differences between smaller and larger churches are included in appendix 2.

5. Ibid.

6. Janet I. Tu, "Pastor Mark Packs 'Em In," *Pacific Northwest*, November 30, 2003, 16–40. (Also available at http://seattletimes.nwsource.com/pacificnw/2003/1130/cover.html.)

7. Shannon O'Leary, "The Power List: 25 Most Influential People," *Seattle*, November 2004, 66–67.

8. "Children in Seattle," *Seattle Times*; Egan, "Vibrant Cities Find One Thing Missing: Children."

9. See www.Acts29Network.org.

10. Go to www.reformission.com for free audio files of this conference.

11. For free audio files, go to www.MarsHillChurch.org.

Chapter Seven: Jesus, We're Loading Our Squirt Guns to Charge Hell Again

1. The concept of organizational maturity is taken from Gerber, *The E-Myth Revisited*.

2. Vaughan, *America's Megachurches 2005*, slide 135.

3. For further study, Strauch's *Biblical Eldership* (cited earlier) is very helpful.

4. If you are not familiar with Dr. Piper, perhaps the best place to start is his most popular book, *Desiring God: Meditations of a Christian Hedonist* (Portland, OR: Multnomah, 1996). You can also visit his website for numerous free theological resources and some great preaching, www.desiringgod.org.

5. Barna, "Twentysomethings Struggle to Find Their Place."

6. Ho, "Just 33 Percent in State Attend Church"; O'Connell Killen, *Religion and Public Life in the Pacific Northwest*; Gossman, "Charting the Unchurched in America"; Zahn, "Washington State May Be Losing Its Faith"; Olson, *The State of the Church in the Seattle Metro Area*, slides 16, 18.

7. Olson, *The State of the Church in the Seattle Metro Area*, slides 36–37.

Apendix One: The Junk Drawer

1. See www.Acts29Network.org.

About the Innovation Series

Leadership Network's mission is to accelerate the impact of 100X leaders. These high-capacity leaders are like the hundredfold crop that comes from seed planted in good soil as Jesus described in Matthew 13:8.

Leadership Network...
- explores the "what's next?" of what could be.
- creates "aha!" environments for collaborative discovery.
- works with exceptional "positive deviants."
- invests in the success of others through generous relationships.
- pursues big impact through measurable kingdom results.
- strives to model Jesus through all we do.

Believing that meaningful conversations and strategic connections can change the world, we seek to help leaders navigate the future by exploring new ideas and finding application for each unique context. Through collaborative meetings and processes, leaders map future possibilities and challenge one another to action that accelerates fruitfulness and effectiveness. Leadership Network shares the learnings and inspiration with others through our books, concept papers, research reports, e-newsletters, podcasts, videos, and online experiences. This in turn generates a ripple effect of new conversations and further influence.

Launched in 2006, the LEADERSHIP NETWORK INNOVATION SERIES presents case studies and insights from leading practitioners and pioneering churches that are successfully navigating the ever-changing streams of spiritual renewal in modern society. Each book offers *real* stories, about *real* leaders, in *real* churches, doing *real* ministry. Readers gain honest and thorough analyses, transferable principles, and clear guidance on how to put proven ideas to work in their individual settings. Real stories, innovative ideas, transferrable truths.

To learn more about Leadership Network go to **www.leadnet.org**

LEADERSHIP ✖ NETWORK*